LILLIAN

David Emery, her fiancé, had known Lillian for one short, but momentous year. He had seen most of her track successes on T.V., but their friendship started with a chance meeting. At the start of the 1970 season he watched her run for the first time. They discussed her plans for the Commonwealth Games and the Olympics to be held in Munich, 1972. But he was to see her build-up for international events beset by illness. She had difficulty keeping to her training schedule, yet refused to think of pulling out. When he learned she had cancer, after the shock and misery, he was left with an unshakeable belief. This had been sent to test her, not to destroy her. She was to be an example to others. She had been singled out to inspire people to beat cancer.

TO LILLIAN

LILLIAN

David Emery

CORONET BOOKS
Hodder Paperbacks Ltd., London

Copyright © 1971 by David Emery
First published by Hodder & Stoughton Ltd., 1971
Coronet edition 1972
Second Impression 1972
Third Impression 1972

Printed in Great Britain
for Coronet Books, Hodder Paperbacks Ltd.,
St. Paul's House, Warwick Lane, London, E.C.4,
by Richard Clay (The Chaucer Press), Ltd.,
Bungay, Suffolk.

ISBN 0 340 15695 3

ACKNOWLEDGMENT

The Board family and David Emery would like to thank Marea Hartman and Bowaters Ltd; Jack Solomons, Alex Alexander and the World Sporting Club; London Olympiades; *The Daily Mail*; and the overwhelming generosity of the public for the help given by them to Lillian in the last few weeks of her life.

Also Melvyn Watman, Editor of *Athletics Weekly*, Cliff Temple of the *Sunday Times,* and Alistair Aitken, for their help in compiling statistics and tape recording conversations used in the book.

CONTENTS

PART ONE

PART TWO

ILLUSTRATIONS

between pages 48 and 49

Key to Acknowledgments

1 Edward Fry
2 *Middlesex County Times*
3 E. D. Lacey
4 *Kentish Mercury*
5 Keystone Press Agency Ltd
6 *The Sun*
7 Press Association
8 Mark Shearman
9 *Daily Express*
10 *Daily Mirror*
11 Tony Duffy
12 K. D. Williams
13 *Evening Standard*
14 Derek Rowe Ltd
15 *Sunday Mirror*
16 Associated Newspapers Ltd
17 Associated Press Photo

PART ONE

1

THE FINAL TRIBUTE

It was cold that morning of Thursday, January 21st, 1971. Windy and with a sharp bite in the air that reminded us of those winter weeks in Bavaria. We were nervous, too, both of the emotion that lay ahead in the next few hours and the sense of finality. So we sat quietly as the big car moved slowly through the thick London traffic. We saw the people lining the approach ways and steps of St Paul's Cathedral soon after we turned into Ludgate Hill. Hundreds of them, some we recognised and so many more we didn't; passers-by and strangers waiting to join in a final tribute to the girl we had all loved in different ways.

St Paul's. Before that day little more than an historical monument to me—built by Christopher Wren between 1674–1710 after the Great Fire of London; burial place of Wellington and Nelson; the setting for memorial services for royalty and statesmen. Now it was being used to honour the daughter of an ordinary working man. Lillian Barbara Board, the girl next door who ruled the world in athletics and captured a nation with her charm and courage.

The well of the cathedral which had looked so vast and deserted when we had discussed service arrangements the previous week was now packed. The celebrity list, headed by the Lord Mayor of London, was filled with sports personalities and officials. International athletes, led by team captain David Hemery, acted as ushers and the Royal Family was represented by Harold Abrahams, chairman of the British Amateur Athletic Board.

It was with a slight feeling of unreality that I took my place at the front. Was all this really being done for the Lillian Board I had known and loved? Not the athlete but the girl. The one with whom I had sipped shandy in country pubs, thrown pebbles at the seaside and eaten hamburgers and chips in a Wimpy bar.

We sat there in a line. Lillian's father George first, then her mother Frances, her twin sister Irene and myself. Nearby were Lillian's brother George, with his wife Marilyn, and Marea Hartman, the manager of the British women's athletics team, who had proved such a fine friend in the recent months. For us it was the end of a so-brief circle. Lillian, baptised in St Paul's Church, Durban, had come to rest twenty-two years later and six thousand miles away at St Paul's, London. And, as we stood for the hymns, knelt for the prayers and sat for the readings I could sense the others doing as I was and glancing at the lofty dome and galleries with a feeling that Lillian was watching; and willing her to appear.

Religion had ceased to make sense for me once Lillian died and I felt a certain sympathy for the Dean, the Very Reverend Martin Sullivan, whose duty called on him to offer an explanation. He urged us to think of Lillian as being close to Jesus; the suffering over. Perhaps in months to come these thoughts would give us comfort. But I knew that at this time words, no matter how sincere, could do little to ease the grief of Frances and George, parents robbed of a loving daughter, or Irene, a twin suddenly standing alone.

It was with the same awful emptiness I had felt at the cremation in Putney a fortnight earlier that I stood to leave at the end. But as I turned I saw the people—for the second time, but as if for the first. Almost two thousand of them. And I realised fully that this was no private loss mourned by a handful of people, it was shared by the country. If there was any consolation in Lillian's illness and death I found it in that moment. For it had shown us in a way that would never otherwise have been possible just how much she had meant to millions.

'FROM LITTLE ACORNS . . .'

They made a handsome group as they walked through
Gunnersbury Park in the suburbs of western London. The
father, in his early forties, moved with the youthful spring of
a natural athlete and a slight roll of the shoulders that bore
silent evidence of his war-time naval service. His wife,
blonde and petite, strolled by his side and a little way beyond her their fifteen-year-old son, George, wove skilful
patterns in the grass with his football.

But most of the attention of passers-by was focused on
the two little girls walking hand-in-hand with their parents.
Their fair hair was cropped short and they wore similar
dresses, one pink, the other blue. Obviously twins, and
almost identical. The casual, admiring glances they received
turned to more genuine interest with what seemed to be the
start of a game. The man suddenly let go of the hand of his
daughter in pink. 'O.K., Irene,' he said, 'off you go.'

The little girl started to run at a surprisingly fast speed
and was fifteen yards away from her parents before the
father turned to her sister in blue. 'Right, Lillian, now see if
you can catch her.' Lillian was quickly into her tiny stride,
with her arms held down by her side and hands flapping like
a miniature penguin. But for all the comedy of her style
there was no hiding another factor—she was astonishingly
quick. She had overhauled her sister within a few seconds
and they fell into each other's arms giggling with the
pleasure of it all. It was a game they played regularly and
they enjoyed it: both for the youthful pleasure of running

14

freely and the inborn instinct of competition. But for their watching father, George, it carried a deeper significance. From the time she had first been able to toddle, Lillian had always seemed quicker on her feet than the other children she played with. As she grew this difference was becoming more obvious.

George had already seen his son develop into an outstanding swimmer who had represented his native Lancashire and was later to win an England junior cap at water polo. Irene had also shown an aptitude for the water. With Lillian, he decided, it was to be athletics.

George had developed a strong interest in the sport while at school—thanks partly to his dislike of maths. He had found that athletic training at Ducie Avenue Central School in his home town of Manchester coincided with the hated subject. He lost no time in bringing his talents to the notice of the sports master and went on to represent the school at sprints and the mile. His stamina strengthened through football, cycling and swimming and his eventual work in the building trade. And his natural lightness of foot was improved by a passion for dancing. But he had never been able to spend the time he would have liked on developing his athletic ability. And that he regretted. Now as he watched Lillian chase after Irene, he felt that she, perhaps more than the others, had inherited his characteristics and he promised himself that if she showed any inclination towards the sport he would give her any help and encouragement necessary to make sure she did not waste her talent.

Lillian had been born in Durban, South Africa, on Monday, December 13th, beating Irene in that race, too, by fifteen minutes. The twins' arrival, in Addington Hospital overlooking the Indian Ocean, consolidated the Board colony which had previously numbered father George, mother Frances, son George Alfred, an alsatian named Tina, a budgie and two tortoises.

The family had emigrated twenty months earlier along with friends from Manchester, Herbert Greenwood, his wife Margaret, and two daughters. They bought a plot of land and built adjacent bungalows. Herbert, a welder, was also in the building trade. It was an idyllic life for a while. Their home on the Bluff at Wentworth overlooked the bay and George junior learnt to swim and surf-ride along the miles of white-sanded, unspoilt beaches. Gradually, though, Frances grew homesick and George, too, began to miss aspects of the English way of life. In February, 1950, the family returned to Manchester and Lillian and Irene eventually started school at St Paul's, Wilmslow Road, Withington.

By the time they moved to Ealing at the age of seven, the twins spoke with broad Manchester accents. They were natural targets for the mickey-takers at their new school—Drayton Green—and tried hard to learn the B.B.C. pronunciations of their class-mates. Just how hard George and Frances did not realise until one day Lillian returned from a visit to the dentist and informed them she had had a tooth out by 'garss'. George, despite his fierce love of Lancashire and a typical county pride, encouraged the girls to gain a London accent and was happy they were attending Drayton Green, a school with a reputation for vocal training.

By this time the twins had developed strong individual personalities. Irene was the mercurial one, quick to try her hand at most things and usually just as quick to drop them. Faster on the uptake and faster to temper, she was indisputably the leader of the two. Lillian, extremely placid like her brother, was more of a plodder. But she coupled that with an unswerving determination to succeed in anything she tried, no matter how long it took. Together the twins joined Ealing Swimming Club—as their brother had done a few years previously—became Girl Guides and took up piano lessons.

Irene proved to be an excellent swimmer but, unlike Lillian, she lacked competitive instinct. She found the pre-race nerves and post-race loss of 'friends' if she won too high a price to pay. So often she turned in mediocre performances simply to keep out of competition reckoning and enjoyed her swimming purely for the pleasure of the sport and as a method of keeping fit. Irene also proved a little too wayward for the Guides and was politely asked to leave. Nor did the slow process of piano lessons suit the impatience of her character. Lillian, however, soldiered on to become a fairly accomplished pianist, a conscientious Guide and, after a slow start, a competent swimmer.

Up till then Lillian had always been by far the shyer of the twins. Whereas Irene would play up to company like a veteran music hall entertainer, Lillian would sit quietly in her chair, almost too unsure of herself to say a word. But as she gradually realised that, given time, she could master anything she put her mind to, she grew in confidence. She was given constant encouragement by her English teacher at Drayton Green, Mrs Kathleen Wharton, who quickly spotted the twins' talent for singing and acting and gave them leading roles in a highly successful school concert. For all her mounting belief in herself, though, Lillian retained the basics of her personality which were to endear her to millions. She was open, almost to a fault, and with a youthful naivety that never left her. She was extremely affectionate and trusting. What 'Daddy' said was gospel and she developed in those formative years an unswerving admiration for his judgment which was to be the foundation for their partnership as athlete and coach in later years.

At the age of eleven Lillian and Irene failed their eleven-plus examination and moved to Grange Secondary Modern Girls' School in Ealing. George was not unduly worried about their missing grammar school. 'As long as you learn to speak correctly and politely and carry yourselves well you'll do all right,' he told them.

The twins' natural athletic ability soon asserted itself at '*the* Grange'—as they always liked to call their school. 'It always makes it sound that little more important,' Lillian would tell her friends. They quickly established themselves in the netball team and went on to play in countless tournaments. But as much as they were happy at the school, it had one big drawback—it did not cater for athletics. George grew anxious in case Lillian's major talent would be stifled.

Then, six months after joining Grange, Lillian arrived home one afternoon with an air of excitement. 'Daddy,' she said breathlessly, 'our new P.E. teacher thinks I should be an athlete.'

'Really? When did she tell you this?'

'Today. We were in the gym and she was watching me and then she said she thought I had something. She wants us to meet her on Sunday and go to a running track at Alperton.'

Lillian's talent-spotter turned out to be Sue Gibson, a student teacher and Middlesex county discus champion. She met George and Lillian on the Sunday and took them to enlist with Alf and Mabel Cotton, who ran London Olympiades. Organisation had come to channel Lillian's natural love of athletics and she thrived on the regular training. But her first track success could hardly have been more unplanned.

Frances was then working in the administration department at Hoover's as a part-time secretary and with the arrival of the firm's sports day she took the twins to watch the running. As the youngsters were getting ready for an 80 yards dash, Frances had a sudden thought. 'Go on, Lillian,' she said, 'you can have a go at that.' Lillian was a little shy to start with but finally agreed and lined up in her pink frock and sandals. She won easily, laughing excitedly as she felt the elation of winning for the first time. She was rewarded with a pink needlework box which she used and treasured always.

Lillian trained conscientiously throughout her first summer with London Olympiades and then reverted to swimming during the winter to build strength. George quickly formed a friendship with Alf Cotton, a former international walker and the Olympiades' chief coach.

'You're always coming down here, George,' Alf told him one night. 'Why don't you give us a hand coaching the juniors?'

It was just the chance George had hoped for. 'If you think I'd be any use, I'd jump at it,' he said. 'I think I do know a little about it.'

George recalled that during the war he had studied submarine detection with a Scot named Sam Kellock, who had been a well-known athlete in the Leicestershire area. 'It was fascinating to hear him talk about athletics,' George told Alf. 'We discussed every aspect and most of it stuck . . . even though we did most of our discussing with a glass in one hand.'

But for all his joking, George treated his honorary appointment with deadly seriousness. Lillian might be too young to be burdened by promises of future greatness, but in George's own mind it was already fact—Lillian was going to be the finest athlete in the world and he was going to steer her carefully along the ladder. He searched for and studied every athletic book in his local book-shops—training manuals, biographies, medical opinions—everything was read thoroughly, digested and practised where George thought applicable.

'I always like to keep an open mind on training methods,' George told friends. 'Just because one method has worked for somebody it doesn't mean it will work for anyone. Every athlete's mental make-up is different and training must be geared to that.'

George coupled commonsense with a firm belief in himself. He would read books by world-famous athletic authorities, but never accepted their ideas as sacred. They were simply a basis for thought, a technique to be modified and stamped with Board individuality. In years to come George was to be criticised for handling Lillian's training and not passing her solely to a national coach. But he had the best answers, 'Look,' he would say, 'children at school spend five years preparing to take, say, five G.C.E. O-levels and some of those they're not interested in. I've spent ten years studying just one subject . . . through genuine interest and love for the sport. Doesn't it follow that I must know something about it?'

Lillian's brother, George, visited Alperton running track occasionally to watch her train. But his eyes could not always have been for his sister alone, for he eventually married Marilyn Pickering, another Olympiade athlete and daughter of Bill Pickering, one of the club coaches.

By the age of thirteen Lillian had established a regular place in the club's junior relay team. The other girls, Celia

Besser, Sue Hopper and Anne Pickering, Marilyn's younger sister, were two years older. They had an excellent season in 1962, winning all before them until they were pipped for victory by a controversial decision in the national junior championships. That season Lillian also ran a few individual 100 and 150 yards.

George, as always carefully charting her course, entered her for the 100 yards in the George French Trophy at Chiswick. He was sure she had a fine chance of winning, a feeling which seemed justified when Lillian clocked 11·8 in the heats, and shared the fastest time with a girl called Jackie Harrison. But Lillian faded in the final which followed twenty minutes later and finished fourth to Jackie Harrison, who won in 11·7. George carefully hid his disappointment as he probed for a reason afterwards.

'You didn't feel tired, did you?' he asked Lillian.

'No, but I was a little full.'

'Full?'

'Well, yes. There wasn't a lot of time before the final and I had to eat my sandwiches and drink my lemonade a little bit quickly.' Then, seeing the look of astonishment on her father's face, she added as a half apology, 'But Daddy, I was so hungry.' It was the beginning of an appetite which became almost a thing of wonder in the Board household.

'Honestly Lillian, anyone would think you were preparing for a siege,' her mother would tell her as she made for bed each night armed with sandwiches, cake, fruit and bottles of pop.

'That's all right,' George said, digging a bit deeper for the housekeeping. 'The engine won't run without fuel.'

Besides developing her style as a sprinter, Lillian branched into long jumping during 1962. Within a few weeks she was clearing fifteen feet and that caught the eye of Ken Woolcott, a long jump coach attached to Middlesex Ladies, who shared the training facilities at Alperton. George welcomed Ken's help, for he felt long jumping would be a good diversion for Lillian. She knew she was training to be a runner, so she would be able to relax and enjoy another event to the full. Also, she had obvious potential and it would have been senseless to waste it. Lillian trained throughout the winter and by the following spring had improved vastly, both as a sprinter and a long jumper. Several good early season runs earned her a reputation as one of Middlesex's best up-and-coming athletes and she gained a bit of Press space in the *Middlesex County Times and Gazette*.

By the middle of May most juniors at London Olympiades were preparing for the all-England Schools Championships at Chelmsford, Essex, on July 20th. Ken Woolcott suggested Lillian should enter for the long jump as he felt she had a fair chance of victory. George took his advice—and immediately ran into his first brush with authority. The P.E. teacher at Grange, anxious to use Lillian's sprinting versatility for the good of the team in their one athletic showing of the year, tried to talk George into changing his mind.

'She'll have no chance in the long jump,' she told him. 'She'll have to clear sixteen feet plus to stand any chance of winning.'

The friction mounted and a good friend of George's suggested it would be better to go along with the school's wishes and not be 'an interfering parent'. But George was adamant. 'I don't care what they say. Lillian is going to do the event of my choice. I'm not going to put her in for the sprints and risk a hammering just for the sake of the school. This is a vital time in her whole approach to athletics. Anyway, the school has had nothing to do with Lillian's athletic ability. They can't turn round and start dictating after the hard work we've put in without any help from them.'

George's decision was quickly vindicated. The following week Lillian won the long jump in the George French Trophy meeting at Chiswick Polytechnic with 16 ft 10 in. She was presented with her prize by Peter Wilson, chief sports writer of the *Daily Mirror*, who later sent George a photograph of the occasion with the inscription—'From little acorns . . .'

On June 8th at the Southern Counties Championships Lillian again won the long jump with 16 ft 4½ in. She also finished third in the 100 yards in 11·4 sec after qualifying times of 11·6 and 11·5. Her consistency was proof of her stamina, but the fact that she had won the long jump but been beaten in the sprints strengthened George's belief that they were right to concentrate on long jumping at that stage of the season. Even so, he was still out on a limb with the school who were smarting over his 'high-handedness' and as the all-England championships drew nearer, George could feel the tension rising. He desperately wanted Lillian to win both for personal satisfaction and, more important, to strengthen her trust in his judgment.

The day of reckoning proved to be glorious. The Chelmsford track was bathed in brilliant sunshine as the thirty-nine competing counties paraded Olympic fashion before the start. Lillian, tall and slender and still with the slight awkwardness of a young foal learning to master the power of its natural physique, marched proudly behind the Middlesex colours, carried by David Travis, future Europa Cup javelin champion. It was an inspiring moment for George. In his mind he could picture the massive electronic score-board and a little way behind the picnicking spectators he could see the Olympic flame burning brightly. He joined the small group around the long jump as the competition began. Lillian's first jump was around 16 ft. Her next four jumps were a similar length—good efforts, but not enough to put her into contention for the title and vindicate George's decision. She had just one attempt left, and George almost willed her through the air as she took off. The measuring tape came out . . . and out again for a check. Lillian had cleared 17 ft 3 in—a personal best, and easily enough to clinch the gold medal. In her first major competition she had shown her ability to rise to the occasion and also her fierce competitive spirit that made her refuse to consider defeat until an event was completely over.

The following week Lillian finished second in the junior long jump in the W.A.A.A. national championships at Watford with 17 ft 5¾ in—it was a defeat for which she gained revenge in the Southern Inter-Counties meeting at Ilford, Essex, at the end of the season. She won with a leap of 17 ft 8½ in—a meeting record and the best jump of the season by a junior.

Lillian had tasted true success for the first time and she thrived on it. But it brought in its wake a sharp lesson about life. She noticed it first at school. Any ticking off from teachers would invariably be ended with 'Just because you think you're good at athletics, don't think that cuts any ice here.' And gradually she found a difference in attitude among some girls at the track. Where at one time they had been friendly rivals now they were just rivals.

'Jealousy,' George told her. 'Try not to let it worry you. Just take it as a compliment.'

During the winter of her fifteenth birthday Lillian trained on Tuesdays and Thursdays at an Alperton track 'flood-lighted' by paraffin lamps. George stepped up her work rate with a view to trying some 220 yard races in the coming season. Lillian would then be an intermediate and would find herself competing with girls of up to seventeen. George felt this would be her most difficult period. He knew some girls put on weight rapidly during those years, others lost interest because of boy friends and many found they hadn't the mental toughness to maintain good level competition week after week. But he had few fears that Lillian would not come through it all right.

Lillian, by then, had begun to appreciate her potential and had her eyes firmly set on an international vest. She gave up swimming and piano lessons to concentrate on ath-letics and her attitude to training revealed the make-up of a champion. She would look around on training nights and notice some athletes chatting in groups or making half-hearted attempts to go through schedules.

'I can't understand why some of them don't take it more seriously,' she would tell her father. 'What's the point of doing athletics if you're not aiming to be the best?'

George explained that for many club members athletics were just a way of keeping fit or a substitute for a youth club where they could meet friends. Lillian took the point, but it was a way of thinking she could never fully understand. In fact, her only complaint about training in those days was that she wanted to do more. George carefully channelled her eagerness. 'You want to be at your best when you're a woman, not a youngster,' he told her. 'This is a woman's sport. True, you can get good results from girls, but how often do they last? I don't believe in running the guts out of willing kids. You have to wait until they are mentally and physically mature.'

Lillian and George had decided to cut down on long jump competition during the coming season and concentrate on sprinting. This move was unwittingly helped when Lillian developed some minor trouble in her right instep.

'It could be because she is hitting the take-off board too hard,' Ken Woolcott told George. 'But anyway, she is too great a runner to risk aggravating the injury through long jumping.'

It was the end of serious jumping competition for Lillian, but two years later, in one of her rare appearances in that event, she proved her world class potential by leaping almost effortlessly 19 ft 1½ in.

Her first meeting of the 1964 season was in the Willis Trophy at Woodside Stadium, Watford. She won the 100 yards in 11·3, her first-ever 220 yards in 26·2 and completed the hat-trick in the relay. The quality of the competition was rising all the time. Lillian was lining up weekly with girls who were later to become the backbone of the British team.

One fairly representative field was in the Southern Counties Championships 100 yards at Chiswick in June. Lillian finished third in the final behind Christine Moore and Barbara Jones, both of whom were second year intermediates. Behind her came Jackie Harrison, Della James, Sheena Willshire and Angela Birch. Besides Lillian, four of the girls in the race—Barbara, Della, Sheena and Angela—went on to become internationals.

Lillian's confidence, which had been growing steadily, rocketed overnight. She had proved that in her first year as an intermediate she could hold her own with the elite over a distance she realised was not her best. George was already gearing her training to 220 yards, with a view to eventual

44os and probable 88os. Her new-found belief in herself showed most in her relationship with Irene. Until then Irene had always been her 'protector', the friendly boss both at school and home. Now Lillian developed a firm will of her own and conquered her natural shyness of people.

Along with the triumphs, though, 1964 brought another experience for Lillian—she finished last in a race for the first time. It happened at a firm's sports day at Beckenham. Lillian had been invited to run in the 100 yards and arrived to find she was competing on an improvised grass track. She trooped down for the start with the rest of the girls and then stood to one side waiting for the customary draw for lanes. It was not until she turned round a few seconds later to see the rest of the girls ready in position that she realised there was to be no draw. Her choice of lane, by now, rested between the inside or outside track—and both were caked in soft, undulating mud for the first ten yards. Lillian was left wading at the start and never recovered. It was a defeat which did not upset her, though, for she had a logical reason for it. This, in fact, was a corner-stone of George's coaching code. 'As long as there's a reason for losing it's all right,' he would tell her. 'But we will never try to make excuses.'

The race also provided Lillian with another lesson in her athletic education: Never allow the opposition to take advantage of your good nature. Be ruthless in competition and make sure that if there are any advantages going it's you that has them. And be on your guard against gamesmanship.

The following July Lillian entered the all-England School Championships 100 yards at Copthall Stadium, Hendon. The meeting was watched by Prince Philip, who landed on the field in a red helicopter. Lillian finished fifth in her final behind Christine Moore, but with the same time as the second girl. Again George was not disappointed for he felt there was a good reason.

Until a couple of weeks before the championships Lillian had been trying to improve her starts. She had concentrated on technique rather than speed from the blocks and consequently in the all-England championships had given the other girls at least a yard at the start. She had recovered well, to come through strongly at the finish. This had pleased George, for in the early days over 100 yards Lillian had 'tied-up' near the finish—not through fatigue but because of sheer determination to go faster. George had worked hard to channel this natural fighting spirit, for at that time it was doing more harm than good. Now, it seemed, Lillian had matured sufficiently to be able to build up speed while still running smoothly.

With a fast-rising star on his hands George was naturally bombarded with well-meaning advice from all manner of athletic followers, experts or otherwise. One suggestion that was particularly popular was that George should try to cut down Lillian's stride length, which was an exceptionally long 7 ft 6 in. It was felt this would help her run more fluidly. George agreed that this might be common sense but refused to do anything about it. 'Lillian's still young,' he would tell the critics. 'We want her to be at her best when she's mature. At the moment her long stride may be a bit of a handicap but when she's got the power to use it properly it will be a tremendous asset.'

Lillian's training for the 200 yards was gradually being stepped up and it showed dividends at the Gibson Trophy meeting at Ilford in the September. She won in 25·5 sec, clipping ·7 off her previous best. It was a fantastic improvement, but one which some people felt might be a flash in the pan. Lillian's chance to prove them wrong came in September at Southend in a race against seniors.

Lillian was nervous about taking on much older opposition and was a little disappointed about drawing the outside lane in only her third attempt at the distance. George, in readiness for just such an occasion, had made sure most of Lillian's training starts were practised in the outside lane to minimise its psychological disadvantages. He emphasised to Lillian that she could use her own pace judgement from that position and she was already feeling better about it when Bill Fisher, the Olympiade coach who had become one of the family's best friends, ended any remaining doubts with his usual down-to-earth reasoning.

'Don't worry, girl,' he said. 'You're in front until some-body passes you.'

Lillian, in fact, stayed in front until almost the final yard when she was caught by Irene Gould, a schools inter-national. It was a fine run, made all the more satisfying by Lillian's time of 25·5, which consolidated her previous im-provement. The Southend meeting was the last on the London Olympiade calendar, but Lillian was still so full of running that George felt it was an ideal time to experiment. For months he had been telling her she would one day be a world class half-miler. Now was the time to prove it. He entered her as a guest competitor for the Middlesex Ladies club championships 880.

'Gosh, Daddy,' Lillian told him as they discussed the race, 'one hundred and fifty yards seems a long way at the moment.'

'Yes, I know,' George reassured her. 'But the half mile will combine your speed with the stamina you have built up in training. Everyone thinks you are just a sprinter, they don't realise just how strong you are. In the past half-milers have been girls who couldn't make the top at sprinting—but you can do both.'

Lillian looked at him wide-eyed, almost in awe of his belief in her capabilities, and answered with the usual air of naivety that made George want to reach out and hug her, 'Do you reckon, Daddy?' It was gullibility to a degree. But George was feeding her no false promises, and deep down Lillian knew that. Everything he had said so far had come true. There was no reason to doubt it would not be so in the future.

George ran that 880 a thousand times in his mind during the week leading up to the big day and by the time it arrived Lillian knew her tactics off by heart. No one at the meeting took Lillian's entry very seriously. Middlesex Ladies had two promising girls in the event, Jane Caffall and Ken Woolcott's daughter, Joanna. Both were specialist half-milers. What chance did a sprinter and one-time long jumper stand against them? As the girls lined up for the start a couple of the spectators called out to Lillian telling her to go out fast at the gun.

'She's bound to fade sooner or later,' one of them told his friend. 'So she might as well set a fast pace so the winner can have a good time.'

Lillian did go out fast and sped round the first bend as if on the opening leg of a 4 × 110 relay. But as soon as she hit the back straight she slowed almost to walking pace—as George had instructed. After a few more yards Joanna Woolcott reluctantly took up the running and Lillian tucked in behind her. So far the tactics had worked. Everyone had been so sure Lillian would lead around the first lap that they did not know how to deal with this new situation. The first 440 was extremely slow and George, standing anxiously on the edge of the track, began to relax. This was just what he had wanted, for he knew none of the other girls could live with Lillian if she was still relatively fresh when they hit the final 200 yards.

The order stayed the same as the girls reached the back straight for the second time. Lillian had been told to make her effort twenty yards from the last bend, win the inside lane, and then hold whoever challenged on her shoulder until she reached the straight. It went like clockwork. Lillian kicked at exactly the right time and swept into the lead. Jane Caffall went after her and Lillian slowed to allow her to draw alongside. But once she got that far Lillian matched her pace for pace, making her run wide round the bend. Then, as they went into the home straight Lillian changed gear to cover the last 100 yards in a fraction below her normal sprinting time and win easily.

The time was a slow 2 min 30·8, but that meant nothing. The important thing was that Lillian had won her first tactical race over a totally unfamiliar distance—the distance which five years later in Athens was to provide her with her greatest triumph.

PRAISE FOR A GIRL

Apart from her father, George, the person to have the biggest influence on Lillian's athletics career was Mary Rand (now Mary Toomey), triple medallist at the Tokyo Olympics. Mary, like Lillian a member of London Olympiades, was in her prime during 1965 and was held in almost god-like awe by the younger members of the club. Lillian was no exception and would tug George's arm excitedly whenever she saw Mary arriving at Alperton for an evening training session. This was fairly infrequent as Mary lived some distance away and did most of her training at a local track. Lillian, with her blonde hair and blue eyes, could have been taken for Mary's younger sister and that, in fact, was the kind of relationship they had.

Shortly after the start of the 1965 season Mary asked Lillian her best 220 time.

'I've just run 25·4,' she told her.

'When you break twenty-five seconds I'll buy you a ring like this one,' Mary said, showing Lillian a platinum ring she had just been given.

Ten days later at Oxford Lillian clocked 24·7 and Mary was quick to keep her promise. 'It just shows what bribery can do,' Lillian joked with her father, delighted both by the present, which she always treasured, and her vast improvement on the track.

As Lillian matured, her relationship with Mary broadened into friendship; friendship based on mutual admiration. Lillian felt Mary was the finest woman athlete ever to represent Great Britain. She also respected the way Mary retained her powerful femininity despite the rigours of training and her almost masculine approach to competition. Lillian had always been particular over her appearance, preferring to wear the fashion of the day rather than slop around in what some athletes considered the uniform of the sport, jeans and tee-shirt. Now, watching Mary, she vowed she would always try and stay first a woman, second an athlete. Her equipment at Athletic meetings always included her hair rollers, lacquer, deodorant and talc and her blue eye shadow became as distinctive on the track side as her blonde hair.

Mary, in return recognised Lillian's tremendous potential. 'Just watch her,' she would tell the Press. 'In a couple of years she's going to be the greatest.' To Lillian she would say, 'I'm billed as the Golden Girl of Athletics. Soon you're going to be taking over that title from me. And they'll have to find a few new ones for you as well, because you're going to be better than I ever was.' It was heady praise for a young girl, but Lillian's natural modesty plus her no-nonsense family background made sure her feet always stayed firmly on the ground. She enjoyed Mary talking that way but told herself to take it as flattery, not as fact.

As well as boosting Lillian's confidence, Mary also gave her the benefit of her vast competition experience and advice on how to behave in front of the Press and public.

'Even when you're at the top there'll be times when you are beaten,' Mary told her. 'You've got to make sure that you keep smiling, even though deep down you feel like strangling someone. It's easy to be a good winner, being a good loser takes real character.' They were words Lillian always remembered, although her own personality would have made it difficult for her to be anything other than gracious in defeat.

Mary, too, had had her fair share of the cattiness that went hand-in-hand with an attractive, successful woman athlete. 'It's just the way of the world,' she would say to Lillian. 'You have to learn to rise above it otherwise it will make you really miserable.'

Lillian was given a sharp reminder of Mary's advice during one of her early international meetings overseas. She had done well on the track and was happily getting ready for the reception in the evening when one of her 'team-mates', watching her meticulously apply her make-up, said sarcastically: 'Oh, Lillian, you do look beautiful.'

'Thanks,' said Lillian. 'I always like a second opinion.'

As well as starting her long relationship with Mary Rand, 1965 also brought Lillian an introduction to Denis Watts, the national coach who had advised Olympic 800 metre gold medallist Ann Packer and Britain's fastest-ever woman sprinter Dorothy Hyman.

It happened in the April, when Lillian was invited to attend a coaching course at Crystal Palace along with leading young athletes from all parts of the country. Her coaches on the course were Olympic silver medallists Robbie Brightwell and John Cooper, Ann Packer, by then Mrs Brightwell, and Denis Watts. They impressed on Lillian what George had always told her: that you got out of the sport only what you were prepared to put into it—and for six days they showed just what could be 'put into it' with as tough a training programme as Lillian had faced. And she loved it. She loved being with people who were as obviously dedicated to the sport as she knew by then that she was; and she thrived on the hard work. It was without doubt the finest coaching course she was ever to attend and she returned home doubly determined to reach the top.

Her home-coming was eagerly awaited by George and Frances, for at the same time as her course had started Irene had gone to Neustadt in West Germany with Ealing Swimming Club. The house seemed strangely quiet and empty with the twins away for the first time and George's diary, in which he charted Lillian's athletic progress, reflected this feeling. It read in daily succession, 'Counting the days' . . . 'Getting nearer' . . . and then on St George's Day, April 23rd, 'All are safely gathered in.'

Lillian had been gathered in only a couple of days when a letter arrived from Denis Watts. He told George how impressed he had been by Lillian's capacity for work and her attitude towards athletics. He ended, 'I am sure she will eventually make a very fine 400 metre runner. If there is any way I can help, please let me know.'

George received the letter with mixed feelings. First, he was delighted that a national coach should be interested in Lillian, for he knew that coaches were too busy to bother with people they were not almost certain would make the grade. Second, from Denis's comments George realised he had been steering Lillian on exactly the right lines. He was just a little worried, though, that he might be pressed to put her training completely in the hands of a national coach. His relationship with Lillian was such that he felt it was in her best interest for him to continue the day-to-day supervision of her training. But he was delighted to accept any help Denis might be able to offer and replied, telling him so.

Meanwhile, Lillian continued to make excellent progress in a season which saw the start of her great rivalry with Della James, an attractive, dark-haired sprinter who had just joined London Olympiades from Portsmouth Athletic Club and was later to run for Britain in the Mexico Olympics. The keenness of the competition between them helped both make rapid improvement on their performances and happily they managed to remain friends for most of the time.

Their first major confrontation came in the All-England Schools Championships at Watford. Lillian had hoped to compete in the 880 but Middlesex county officials asked her to run in the 150 yards and relay to strengthen the team and this time George did not object to his plans being altered. Lillian won her 150 yard heat in a championship record 16·6 despite a powerful head wind. She won her semi-final the following day in 16·9, but complained of feeling a little groggy and developed a heavy nose bleed a few minutes before the final. George advised her not to run, but she insisted on going ahead and Della beat her by a stride in 16·6. George expected her to be deeply disappointed by the defeat. Instead she told him, 'I feel so happy that Della's won an all-England gold. I know how great I felt when I won the long jump title as a junior.'

Della was also coached by her father, Douglas James. So

George now had a double family score to settle. He was sure the chance would come in the Women's A.A.A. intermediate championships at Harlow the following week. Della and Lillian were due to clash in the 220. There was a strong wind blowing across the first bend in the 220 by the time they settled in their blocks for the final. George had instructed Lillian to use her strength and make an all-out effort over the first 150 yards and then try and hang on. Lillian did exactly as she was told and hit the home straight with a clear lead. Della made a tremendous effort to close the gap and drew nearer inch by inch over the last fifty yards. They went over the line almost together and were both credited with 25·8.

It was a near thing, but Lillian was sure she had just taken the verdict, a feeling strengthened when Della turned to her immediately afterwards and said sportingly, 'Congratulations, I knew you had me when I saw the seat of your pants.' George was in the middle of giving Lillian a victory hug when the loudspeaker announcement was made, 'First, Della James, London Olympiades, 25·8; second Lillian Board, London . . .'

George was amazed and then furious. He hurried to the finish and found the officials had disagreed, but the majority had voted for Della. He was all set to make an official protest but Lillian stopped him and added without a trace of bitterness, 'It's not worth it. I know I won and so does Della. In fact, I feel a bit sorry for her.' George eventually agreed. 'We'll make damn sure it doesn't happen in the future, though,' he said. 'We'll work that much harder and get you so much better that there will never be any doubt again.'

The end of August brought Lillian's first trip abroad. Southend Athletic Club had been invited to compete in Krefeld, West Germany, and asked Lillian along as a guest competitor to strengthen their team. Lillian's team-mates included Southend's Ann Wilson, who in the next couple of years was to join Lillian as one of the most exciting young women athletes in Britain. Lillian was thrilled with the trip and discovered for the first time her love of travel, and the excitement of competing against foreign opposition. And there was no doubting her success. By the end of the season her best marks were

Event	Best Performance	Overall position in British intermediate list
100 yards	10·9 sec	First
150 yards	16·6 sec	Equal first
220 yards	24·7 sec	Second
880 yards	2 min 25·5 sec	Sixth
Long jump	19 ft 0¼ in	Second

It was a remarkable range of ability and one which she increased at her first indoor meeting at Cosford, Wolverhampton, in November. She won the 60 yard sprint in 7·2 sec and the 330 yards in 42 sec. Her performance prompted the London *Evening News* to give her her first major Press notice. Under a headline LILLIAN'S DILEMMA athletics correspondent Ron Lindstead wrote:

> The recently ended athletics season has left 16-year-old Lillian Board of London Olympiades A.C. with a problem.
> Lillian has turned out to be an athlete with almost an embarrassment of diverse talent . . . Sprinter, middle-distance runner or long jumper, Lillian will now have to decide in which to specialise in order to reach the top.

But Lillian's mind was already made up. The following year she would be a senior and able to compete for the first time over 440 yards. It was the chance she had been waiting for. George and Denis Watts had exchanged several more letters during the season and now, with the coming of winter, Denis sent him a schedule for track work and weight training. George had already been thinking that Lillian should start using weights to increase her sprinting power. He had looked around to find somewhere for her to go and

34

found the answer almost on his doorstep. It came through Lillian's brother George and his fierce passion for folk music.

George, an accomplished guitarist and amateur song writer, had joined Ealing Folk Club while in his early teens. He teamed up with a couple of other young guitarists, Alan Young and Don Partridge, who was later to become a national pop idol with his hit song 'Rosie', and together they toured most of the local folk clubs. During these years George became friendly with John Barter and John Wrightson, folk music enthusiasts who lived about half a mile away from his home in Ealing. They lived together in a big, rambling house and after a while George started going round there every Sunday morning for a sing-song. The 'two Johns', as George described them to his father, had another hobby besides folk music—weight-lifting. George had trained with them occasionally to help his swimming and football. So when his father mentioned he was trying to find somewhere for Lillian to do weights, George had the immediate answer.

It was the start of a long friendship between Lillian and the two Johns. John Barter, aged about 50, became known as Big John and John Wrightson, 26, was Little John. They fussed over Lillian like two hens with a chick. Usually they flopped around their house in jeans and sweat shirts. But the nights Lillian visited them they dressed up almost in Sunday best as a mark of their respect.

'Lillian always looked immaculate,' Big John recalls. 'She took a great pride in her appearance even at that early age and this grew more important to her over the years. She was always vivacious and we used to really look forward to her sessions with us, three nights a week.'

The Johns had a huge selection of records and most of Lillian's exercises were done to a background of stereophonic pop. The men became two of Lillian's staunchest fans and admirers and often visited Alperton track to watch her other training. They even tried some athletics themselves.

'Lillian had that kind of inspiring influence,' John Barter

says. 'She made you feel you wanted to try and emulate her.'

Gradually Lillian's strength increased, but the exercises were so designed that there was never any danger of her ending up as a muscle-bound Amazon. They merely toughened her existing muscles, developed her stamina and helped trim her figure to a film star's 36-24-36.

By now, George was having regular correspondence with Denis Watts. He reported weekly on Lillian's progress and in return was sent more schedules. He tried to keep as closely as possible to Denis's suggestions, but varying daily factors such as the weather, Lillian's state of health and reaction to the previous day's training, forced him to use his own improvisation as he had in the past.

George had passed an honorary coaching course for sprinting and middle distance and relay running the year before, and could have gone on for higher examinations and qualifications. But he felt no need to prove himself. He knew his knowledge of coaching was as good as anybody's in the country without having a piece of paper to prove it. And as long as Lillian continued to make her expected progress he was quite happy. He was an unostentatious figure at the track, refusing to dress up in what many coaches felt were essentials for their trade; peak cap, bright blazers and an ever-present whistle hanging round their necks. 'They're all done up like frogs in blotting paper,' George would say. 'You wouldn't catch me togged up like that.'

Midway through Lillian's winter training the Women's A.A.A. Indoor Championships were held at Cosford, Wolverhampton. Lillian entered for the 60 yards dash and showed the full benefit of her improved strength by finishing second in the final to Daphne Arden, known as 'The Queen of the Boards' because of her tremendous performances at indoor meetings. Both clocked 7·1 sec. George was delighted. Everything was going as planned and pointing to Lillian's best-ever season. His hopes were realised in Lillian's opening race on April 23rd. She won the 100 yards at an inter-club meeting at Southall in 10·6 to equal the British record. It was wind-assisted and so was not put forward for ratification. But as George told Lillian afterwards, 'At least it shows your legs can go that fast. And anyway, the 100 isn't the distance we're really interested in.'

That same afternoon Lillian entered for her first attempt at the 440. The wind was still blowing strongly, gusting across the final bend of the track. It was obviously not a day when Lillian would set a good time. But this worried neither her nor George. The important thing was to get her initiated over the distance. Several experts had told George he should instruct Lillian to run the first 300 yards flat out to use her sprinting speed and then try and hang on for the last 140 yards. But George disagreed. He did not want Lillian to finish exhausted and in possible distress in case it frightened her from the event. He told her to run within herself until she hit the home straight and then strike for home.

Avril Usher, the British international, was a clear favourite for the race and soon showed why. By the time they reached the last 100 yards she had opened a huge gap. But then Lillian tapped the strength she had held in reserve to cut her lead enormously. Avril won in 57·8 and Lillian finished a relaxed and confident second in 58·1. It was a fine introduction to what many athletic experts considered 'the killer event'. Lillian had proved her stamina and speed and, more important, she now had a firm belief in her capabilities over the distance.

'I know I can go much faster than that,' she told George afterwards—and proved it three weeks later with a 57·2 in her club championships.

Lillian thrived on the 440, partly because she realised it was a race in which she could bring all her guns to bear and partly because it gave her a break from the cat and dog fight of the short sprints. In London Olympiades alone she was up against internationals Mary Rand, Janet Simpson, Della James and Barbara Jones over the 100 and 220. The rivalry was intense and so was the resultant tension. In the 440 she was competing against more mature opposition, established 440 runners, and so she had nothing to lose.

With this in mind George decided she should concentrate

37

on the 440 in the Southern Counties Championships. But, fast learning the art of gamesmanship, he put her name down for the 100 and 220 as well, just to keep the opposition guessing. It turned out to be an exhausting afternoon for Lillian. She ran in three 440s in the space of a few hours—quite an ordeal for a seventeen-year-old who was still a novice at the race. But she came through it well, clocking 58·9 in her heat, 58·6 in the semi-final and 57·3 for third place in the final behind two of Britain's top quarter-milers, Deidre Watkinson and Avril Usher.

Weight training had played a big part. For, as George stressed to Lillian, an athlete is only as strong as his weakest set of muscles. If his body isn't properly balanced his running form disintegrates as soon as fatigue starts. This never happened to Lillian. She always maintained co-ordination no matter how tired she was at the end of a race.

With the coming of the Women's A.A.A. Championships at the White City on July 1st and 2nd Denis Watts, who had been in regular contact with George, suggested Lillian should enter for the 100 and 220. His reasoning was influenced by the fact that Lillian had run a 25·1 220 the previous week to smash a ten-year-old meeting record at the Middlesex Schools Championships. But George had seen that only as a speed sharpener for future 440s. He told Denis so and added, 'Lillian is quite happy about entering for the quarter-mile in the Women's A.A.A.s. We feel the event is tailor-made for her and are sure she will do well—you wait and see.'

Denis didn't have to wait long. With her amazing ability to raise her performance when it mattered, Lillian made a mockery of her previous form to storm through her heat with 55·7—a full one and a half seconds off her previous best. It was an amazing breakthrough. But more was to follow. She tore out of her blocks in the semi-final to pass the 220 yard mark in 25·2—just one-tenth outside her best for that distance—and then hung on to finish fourth with 54·6. It was a time which would have earned her fourth place in the Tokyo Olympics three years earlier. But the standard of competition, with many of the world's top quarter-milers in the field, was such that she did not even qualify for the final. But Lillian had ample compensation. It was the fastest 440 ever run by a seventeen-year-old in Europe and only one-tenth of a second outside the world's best for the age group. Also it was faster than the time clocked by Joy Grieveson, Britain's number one quarter-miler, in winning the other semi-final.

Lillian had gone in for the championships knowing they would be used as a basis for team selection for the Commonwealth Games in Jamaica in August. Had she done enough to be selected? Her performances and potential spoke for themselves, but would the selectors risk pitching a virtual unknown into the tension-fraught world of a major Games? The postman came and passed on Monday and the phone stood silent. Lillian said little, but her family could feel her anxiety of doubt. Then on Tuesday it arrived. A white, unspectacular envelope which crystallised and repaid five years of hard work and hope. She had been chosen, along with Joy Grieveson and Deidre Watkinson, to represent England in the Commonwealth 440.

George was out at work when Lillian opened the letter, so in her excitement she telephoned her brother's in-laws, Mr and Mrs Bill Pickering. 'We'll have to tell your father straight away,' Bill Pickering said, picked Lillian up in his car and drove her to Shepherd's Bush where George was working on an underground sewer. 'Someone to see you, George,' one of his work mates called down the tunnel and George emerged unsuspecting into the sunshine to find a radiant Lillian bubbling with the news.

The Amateur Athletic Board, realising Lillian would be apprehensive about making her international debut in such an important competition, decided to blood her the following weekend at a representative 400 metres in Prague. George was walking around a couple of feet off the ground by now and he floated even higher when he heard Lillian's travelling companions to Prague would be Dorothy Shirley, the Olympic silver medallist high jumper who hailed from his native Lancashire, and Mabel Cotton of London Olympiades.

'You could have had only one better person to go with,' he said. 'And I've got to stay here to look after your mother!'

The meeting attracted a huge crowd, mainly because Anna Chmelkova, the Czechoslovak European 400 metre champion, was appearing in her home territory. She was clear favourite, but made two false starts and was disqualified. The girls got away at the third attempt and Lillian, as usual feeling the tension fall away at the echo of the starting gun, quickly built up top speed and then eased down the back straight ready for a finishing burst. As she rounded the final bend well positioned just behind two local girls, she met the full volume of the cheering crowd. It could have been an overawing experience for a young debutante, instead it was an inspiration.

'I pretended they were shouting for me,' Lillian said later after she had cleaved through the opposition to win in 55·1.

As the photographers swarmed round, Lillian, as always, started to push wayward pieces of hair back into place and fiddle with the curls around her temples. The crowd went wild. 'I thought I'd split my shorts,' she said. 'Then I realised the Iron Curtain crowds weren't used to women athletes showing femininity, so I exaggerated it even more.'

Lillian became an overnight celebrity in Prague and was swamped by invitations to compete at other local meetings. She politely refused and returned home as planned. 'There was no point staying on,' she told George, surprising him with the way her thinking had matured. 'I would only have been used to draw crowds as a target for other local athletes to try and knock down.'

Her victory was a perfect preparation for the Commonwealth Games and Lillian left for Kingston, Jamaica, in high spirits. Her room mate for the meeting was Ann Wilson and they quickly formed a firm friendship, partly because of their similar personalities and partly because they were ignored a little by the more established members of the team and made fully aware that they were the newcomers and not, as yet, part of the 'gang'. The arrival of Mary Rand, who had stopped off en route to take part in another meeting, cut through most of this mini-segregation. She welcomed Lillian as a friend, made her feel instantly at home, and drew her and Ann into the team chatter.

Lillian was both impressed and a little frightened by the overall magnificence and aura of the Games: the shirt-sleeved jamboree crowds filling the arena in outrageous kaleidescopes of colour; the sensual, basic music of the steel bands that jangled across the city like mechanised tribal drums, the endless blue sky straight out of a child's painting book, and the heat. 'Boy, this heat,' Lillian told a team official. 'I've never known humidity like it. One day's training is better than a week's crash diet. I just hope it doesn't affect my running.'

She exploded all fears in her qualifying round, winning in 54·7, just one-tenth outside her best. She repeated the time for fifth place in the final. Her selection had been justified and she was rightly proud of her performance. Of the other British girls involved, Joy Grieveson had an off-day and failed to qualify for the final, Deidre Watkinson took the silver medal and Rosemary Stirling, who was representing Scotland, was fourth.

Lillian was elated. But disappointment was to follow. Immediately after she returned from Jamaica the British team for the European Championships in Budapest was announced. Lillian was not among it. The three girls selected for the 400 metres were Grieveson, Watkinson and Stirling. Lillian had even failed to make the reserves. George, though, was not too concerned. He had realised Joy Grieveson would not be dropped just on the basis of one disappointing run and the others had clearly earned the trip.

'Lillian's run thirteen quarters already this season,' he told Frances. 'She would have to run three more to do anything in the Europeans and the competition is very hot. She would stand the chance of getting hammered, which could be very demoralising at this stage. I don't really under stand why she isn't a reserve, though. I think that must be just an oversight.'

The oversight proved embarrassing for the British selectors, when, by no fault of theirs, the start of the

Championships brought something approaching a fiasco. First they discovered Joy Grieveson was injured and unable to compete. Second Anne Smith, the world mile record holder who was due to run in the 800 metres, walked out of the Games village and disappeared. Lillian had ample qualifications to have stepped in for either, had she been a reserve, and the Press were quick to point this out.

Amends were made a few weeks later when Lillian was awarded her full international vest in the Great Britain versus France match at Lille. The British team gave an uncharacteristically sluggish display that day with the result that only a couple of points separated the teams by the time the programme reached the 400 metres. Lillian, walking to the start and well conscious of the importance of her race, was stopped by a team official.

'Lillian, you've got to give it everything you've got,' he told her.

'I always do,' she answered with a tinge of anger. But the damage had been done.

Still annoyed by what she took to be an inference, Lillian blasted from her blocks, covered the first 200 at top sprint and then found she was burnt out by the home straight. She finished last to join the ranks of stars like Mary Rand and Lynn Davies who had similarly 'flopped' in their full international debuts. But despite her defeat, Lillian had still impressed some with her qualities. Neil Allen, athletics correspondent for *The Times*, wrote the following day:

Though she finished last in the 400 metres, 0·4 sec behind Rosemary Stirling, almost as bright a prospect for the future as Ann Wilson may still be Lillian Board, not 18 until December.

She was below her best yesterday afternoon simply because her determination carried her through the first 200 metres at a reckless pace. But Miss Board has the rare capacity to run herself right out.

George, still with his eye firmly fixed on future 800 metres, entered Lillian for two cross country meetings at the start of the winter. She won both, but hated that form of running.

'You think the race will never end,' she said. 'It gets boring and exhausting. On the track you condition yourself to accept pain for maybe fifteen seconds of a 400 metres and thirty seconds of an 800. In cross country it just goes on and on.'

George was delighted by her performances in what had really been only over-distance training. Lillian, too, was glad she had kept in trim, for a week later she was invited to compete in Cuba at a meeting commemorating the Castro revolution. With only the cross country and a few sessions of weight training behind her in the previous three months, she won the 400 in 55·0, two and a half seconds ahead of Hungary's Antonia Munkasci, the European silver medallist. Lillian celebrated her eighteenth birthday on December 13th at a party given for the British contestants by the British Consul. It was a fitting end to a triumphant season.

4

THE COMMENTATOR'S DREAM

George by now was a well-known figure in national athletics and went part way to repaying some of the pleasure he had derived from the sport by becoming an active committee member at London Olympiades. He also made his coaching services freely available for any of Lillian's younger club mates who wanted his advice.

As his interest deepened and his knowledge increased he began to look at the structure of the sport and found what he felt to be an important anomaly. At the end of the 1966 season he attended the annual meeting of the Southern Counties Women's Athletics Association anxious to put it right. His proposal was that the 440 should be added to the national championships list of events for intermediate girls. At that time intermediates could run 880 yards—but not 440. And juniors, who were also barred from 440 competition, were encouraged to take part in cross country events of up to one and a half miles.

'Britain's strength has always been in the longer sprints and middle distances,' he told the meeting. 'It would seem sensible to encourage our girls to take up these events at an early age. At the present moment it's rather like jumping from an O-level course into university.'

To his amazement, the idea was treated almost with scorn by the vast majority of the people there.

'It's a killer race,' someone shouted. 'It's savage to ask young girls to run that distance.'

'I'm talking about intermediates,' George emphasised.

44

'When you consider juniors are doing cross country, surely its ridiculous to stop older girls running a sixth of the distance?'

'They can stop and walk at cross country,' he was told. 'They can stop and walk in the 440 if they want to. Young girls will only run as fast as their training allows, they won't push themselves to exhaustion like older competitors. It would be a gradual acclimatisation to the event.' But as he argued George knew he was already beaten and was preparing to sit down when the final barb was flung by a man who considered himself an athletics' expert.

'That idea might be all right for anyone like Lillian Board who can't run anything else,' he said.

In view of the praise Lillian's range of talents had brought only the previous year George decided it was a remark best left unanswered for fear of regretting later what he might say. Instead he let his proposal be put to a vote and it was thrown out by 70 to 7.

George returned home that night with mixed feelings. He had purposely waited until Lillian had become a senior before raising the question, lest people would think he was just trying to promote his own cause. To do it for completely unselfish reasons and still have it thrown back in his face was doubly distressing. He told Lillian the outcome of the meeting and then consoled himself with the thought, 'Oh well, it just means everybody else will be that much further behind you over the next couple of years. It's their own fault now.'

In his own mind he was certain he was still right. Provided a young athlete was brought along with care and thought, nothing but good could come from an early introduction to their chosen event. Pace-judgement, competition experience and general confidence would be nurtured during those formative years so that when they became seniors and met top level opposition they would be half prepared for the challenge. (In fact 440's for intermediates were introduced in 1969.) George had brought Lillian on with the care of a master gardener for an exotic plant. He had never run her into the ground during training, preferring to ask her to tackle schedules he knew were well within her capabilities rather than push her to the limit. His job, as he saw it, was to build her up, not pull her down with the burden of work. Staleness and boredom in training were dangers he was very much alive to. And for that reason he never advocated vast weekly mileages, but preferred quality repetition work with short recovery intervals.

He was the first to admit, though, that in Lillian he had the perfect pupil. Never once did he have to force her to complete a schedule. More often he would tell her the session was over and she would demand to do more because she didn't feel tired enough. 'A willing horse doesn't need a whip,' was his theory! And all the time he worked on her mental approach to athletics. The four-mile car drive to and from the track was an unbroken conversation. Both Lillian's performances and the form of her rivals were discussed, analysed and evaluated, and often the talk would flow over into the saloon bar of the 'Myllet Arms' which they treated as their 19th hole after training.

George's attempts to build in Lillian the mentality of a champion were helped no end by Denis Watts. His letters were full of constant praise, encouragement and predictions of greatness for the future. 'If I read those letters enough times I'm bloody sure I could go out and win a gold medal,' George joked to Lillian.

But even without George to inspire her, Lillian had already set her targets in her own mind. She wanted an Olympic gold medal and a world record and, in her usual dogged way, she was determined nothing would stop her. The motivation behind these ambitions was contained in a single question and answer.

'Why do you run?' someone asked her once.

'Because I'm good at it,' she said.

And that was almost the complete reason. In atheletics Lillian had found a sphere where she could climb high above those who had left her in their wake academically or materially. It was a kingdom over which she knew one day she could rule. It was an identity for a shy girl who through her own placid sweetness as a child had felt the painful experience of lack of confidence.

At the age of sixteen and a half she and Irene had left the Grange and moved to Chiswick Polytechnic to take a secretarial course. The daily contact with older company increased the lure of a gay social life. Even that could not sway Lillian. Night after night she turned down possible dates on the grounds that training came first. And gradually the mickey-taking started. But her trips abroad and her success on the track had done wonders for her confidence, and whereas at school the jibes had hurt she now turned them aside with a skilful, rapid line of repartee. She enjoyed a normal, steady social life. But it was on her own terms— and that meant athletics first.

Lillian's growing confidence also showed in the way she handled herself during interviews with the Press. Where at one time she had been shy and hesitant, she now controlled the questioning like the chairman of a panel. She put her views clearly and concisely and laced them with her own brand of developing humour. She had long lost the last traces of her Manchester accent and her diction was now clear and perfect apart from a lisp which was an endearment rather than an impediment. She had also learnt, partly from Mary Rand's example, what was expected of her and would stand chatting patiently and sweetly to the Press up to an hour after a gruelling race when more than anything she was longing to get under a shower. She had become, as T.V. sports commentator David Coleman said, 'An interviewer's dream.'

Her blossoming personality brought a change of attitude among her club mates. For in the early years her shyness and dedication to training had been taken as snobbery. She didn't chat much with the girls and they felt she was a little aloof. Now they realised how wrong they had been; the inner Lillian which had been struggling for recognition, began to emerge.

TRIUMPH AT LOS ANGELES

Lillian left Chiswick Polytechnic in the spring of 1967 when she was seventeen and a half and with Irene joined a local staff agency as a temporary. The work was inconsistent, but that suited Lillian. A free week here and there meant she could approach evening training with a fresher mind—and sometimes she needed it, for the training was getting tougher. The previous year her most gruelling session had been 8 × 220 yards with forty-five seconds recovery between each. Now she was tackling 6 × 330 with fifty seconds recovery.

The highlight of the athletics' calendar that year was a Commonwealth versus U.S.A. match in Los Angeles in July. Lillian was anxious to set a fast 440 time early on to put herself in the reckoning for selection. She entered and won a series of races at the start of the season but weather conditions, the state of some tracks, lack of competition and the fact that it was early season brought more and more frustration. She clocked in succession 56·6, 57·5, 57·5, 55·9, 55·7, 55·7 and 56·3. It was encouraging form for that time of year but hardly the sort of performance Lillian felt would warrant selection.

'The times will come,' George reasured her. 'In a month's time you'll be able to run with exactly the same amount of effort for about a two second improvement. The selectors realise this. They know your form last season and the amount of training you've done this past winter.'

Lillian, knowing as always that her father would tell her

Lillian (*right*) and Irene with brother George and father, 1949.

Lillian, aged 5, with the smile which was to become famous.

Grange School netball team. Irene (captain) centre, Lillian back row left.

The family in grandmother's
garden in Manchester.

The London Olympiads Junior
Relay Team, Lillian (*left*),
aged 13.

The George French Trophy meeting, Junior 100 yd. Final 1962.
Lillian came in fourth.

The kind of long jump that won Lillian the All-England title in 1963.

Sunday morning at Alperton. A 16-year-old Lillian showing perfect form.

Janet Simpson hands Lillian her medal for coming second in the 150 yd. All-England Schools meeting at Watford in 1964. The winner was Della James. Margaret Critchley came third.

The athlete and her trainer (*above*) in 1967 keeping fit to music, while Irene looks on (*below*) practising starts at her home track, the West London Stadium, in May, 1970.

Above left. A warm welcome home from her mother after the 1966 Commonwealth Games in Jamaica.

Above right. In 1967 Lillian won the National Championship and eight of her ten international races to become athlete of the year with Lynn Davies.

One golden girl of British athletics taking over from another. Mary Rand (*left*) and Lillian in the 4 × 200 m. relay, Great Britain v. West Germany, 1967.

Lillian at the start of the 440 yd. in the W.A.A.A. Championships, 1967.

The British team who beat the West Germans in the 4 × 200 m. at the White City, 1967. (*From the left*) Mary Rand, Lillian Board, Maureen Tranter, Shena Willshire.

Lillian winning the 440 yd.

Soon after the
start of the
800 m. world
record race in
the W.A.A.A.
Championships
at Crystal
Palace 1968.
Vera Nikolic
leads Pat Lowe
and Lillian
Board.

Lillian is the
first to
congratulate
Vera Nikolic
on her world
record.

The world record
breakers at
Portsmouth, 1968.
(*From the left*)
Maureen Tranter,
Anita Neil, Lillian
Board, Janet
Simpson.

what he believed to be true and not flatter her with empty words, was reassured. But even so, she could hardly have been prepared for the chain of events on Sunday, June 11th.

At the start of the day its importance was divided between the fact that it was her mother's birthday and that Lillian was competing in a 440 at Brighton that afternoon against Anne Smith. That was eclipsed when brother George arrived excitedly at the house to announce he had become a father with a more than bonny 9 lb 1 oz daughter called Lorraine Sarah. In the middle of the congratulations Lillian's father came racing back from the newsagents brandishing the paper. The Los Angeles team was listed—and Lillian was in. Her team-mates for the 400 metres were Una Morris of Jamaica and Judy Pollock, Australian 26-year-old 440 yard world record holder.

Lillian celebrated in the best possible style, scorching to victory in the afternoon in a personal best 54·4. Anne Smith, making a rare appearance over the distance, was second in 56 seconds. She had proved the selectors right. She had also gone part way in convincing herself that perhaps she really was as good as her father was always telling her. But she still had her doubts and looked towards Los Angeles with a question mark.

For George Los Angeles was the next step on the ladder, almost a fait accompli from the beginning of the season. He fostered and shared Lillian's excitement at the thought of the trip. But already he was planning ahead—years ahead. With that in mind he entered Lillian for an 880 at Reading on June 14th. For Lillian it would be a break from the tension of the 440. For him it would be a pointer to the future.

It was Lillian's first try at the distance as a senior and she was up against Pam Piercy, a courageous Yorkshire girl who had been fourth in the European Championships the previous year and was reigning 'Athlete of the Year'. George's tactics were simple. Lillian was to sit on the shoulders of the leaders until the final 220. Then she had to kick for 100 yards, ease up for forty as the other girls tried to catch up, then kick again.

'There's nothing more destroying,' George told her, 'than to flog yourself to death to close a gap only to find as soon as you do it that the girl in front sprints again.'

Lillian translated the words into deeds, winning in 2 min 8·7 sec with Pam Piercy second in 2 min 10·2 sec. George's satisfaction at victory was surpassed only by his pleasure at Lillian's reaction, 'Daddy,' she told him in excited surprise, 'it was so easy . . . so much easier than the 440.'

Everything Lillian did was now news and during the next couple of weeks she had her first real taste of Press pressure. It was centred around her scheduled 440 run in the Women's A.A.A. Championships at the White City on July 1st. On paper Lillian was a clear favourite, her rivals were still struggling to find form. It was the first time she had been expected to win an important competition and she didn't relish the role.

'I'm so nervous about this race,' she confided to her father. 'Everybody will be out to beat me, to say they should have had the Los Angeles trip. I've got everything to lose.'

The strain began to tell. She developed a queasy stomach and went off her food. 'For the first time,' she told Irene, 'I can really understand why you don't like competition. If you used to feel this way every time you swam, I'm not surprised you packed it in.' To make matters worse, Lillian suddenly realised that July 1st was going to fall right at the start of her monthly period. 'I just hope the Press understand,' she told George. 'But they often seem to forget why women athletes show a sudden drop in performances on a particular day.' But, despite everything, Lillian never once considered pulling out, 'I don't care what happens, I'm not going to be thought a coward. And even if I lose I've got the satisfaction of knowing there's a reason . . . not an excuse.'

Lillian won her heat on the Friday night, June 30th, in 55·2, but her fears had been realised. 'It was terribly hard, my legs were so heavy down the home straight,' she told George. 'It's so frustrating when you know you should win, that you can win, but your legs won't answer to what you tell them.'

The next morning she felt worse and George suggested

they went for a drive to Horsenden Hill, a local beauty spot. It was a superb day, and sitting in the shade of a giant elm tree, looking out over the miles of toy-town scenery, George felt that afternoon's race belonged to a different world. Lillian slowly relaxed and together they calmly planned her best possible tactics.

'We know my legs are going to go,' Lillian said. 'So I might as well go out fast and try to hang on.'

'Yes,' George agreed. 'But you've got to go out more than fast, you've got to go as fast as you possibly can.'

With a set goal, Lillian lost some of her nervousness and singlemindedly set about preparing herself for the race. George knew she would do as he had suggested and took particular care over his timing of the first 220. Lillian went out like a hare. 'She's really motoring,' George shouted to Frances as he slammed down the button on his stop-watch. 'Just as we planned.' He took a quick glance at the time and gasped in amazement—24·6. Lillian's personal best for the 220, set earlier that season, was 24·7. But there was still half this race to go.

Lillian hit the straight with a clear lead, but her legs were fading fast. She gritted her teeth, tried to keep some semblance of running form, and almost fell across the tape to beat Mary Green by inches. Both were timed at 55·3. Strangely it was to be Lillian's only national title. A world record run by Vera Nikolic, injury and illness were to foil her three other chances.

*   *   *

LOS ANGELES, California: A Pacific playground of neon lights and night clubs . . . the city chosen by Walt Disney as the setting for his fantasy world of Disneyland. This was to provide Lillian with the background of one of her greatest dramas.

She was accompanied on the trip by Mary Rand and together they captivated the American Press and public. Their blonde good looks, overall femininity and easy, girlish chatter during interviews, was an education to the

American fans, so used to Negro-dominated athletic meetings.

'You dizzy English blondes,' one of the newspaper men told Lillian. 'Jeez, you're something else again.' It was a phrase which delighted Lillian and became one of her party pieces.

Lillian's love of meeting new people and her growing ability to mix in any company, allowed her to fully appreciate the social side of the trip and provided some relaxation from the pre-race tension. But at the times when she was by herself and anxiously considering the kind of performances she would give, her mind harped back to a conversation she had had with George just before she had left for the plane.

'You have absolutely nothing to lose, our kid,' he had told her. 'This is virtually a world championship 400 and nobody expects you to do very much. But I promise you whatever happens you will do a personal best. You have worked hard, you're fit and your true form will show itself, and you may surprise yourself.'

Lillian's best time of 54·4 was the slowest of the field. Three of the other girls were in the 52s. As they walked to the start in blazing sunshine and a temperature of around 100 degrees, the announcer sketched out each girl's history and their times for the event.

'I felt like a poor relation,' Lillian said later. 'I could hardly wait for the gun to go so I could get out and do something about it.'

George and Frances, sitting in a crowded London living room, knew how she would be feeling. The race was being televised on B.B.C. 2 and Alf Cotton had invited them round to his house to watch it. George tried to hide his nervousness with a bit of light-hearted banter, but his hands were gripping the chair tightly as the gun went.

Judy Pollock, in the lane immediately outside Lillian, flew from her blocks. Lillian set off in fast pursuit.

'And there goes young Lillian Board after the world record holder,' commentator David Coleman said excitedly. But as they reached the 200 metre mark Lillian lost contact.

'Board is fading badly now,' said Coleman and a ripple of disappointment ran through Alf Cotton's guests.

'Oh Lillian!' Frances murmured, a question mark in her voice, and George knew that everyone else in the room, apart from him, thought Lillian was outclassed.

'The bloody race isn't over yet,' he cried.

On the Los Angeles track Lillian had reached the final bend. She was last, a couple of yards behind the nearest girls. In her fleeting thoughts she knew what it must look like to onlookers. 'Oh, I can't be last,' she told herself. 'Please don't let me be last.'

Even George was hardly prepared for her sudden acceleration. She overhauled the two girls in front within a few strides. 'She's going to be fourth,' he thought happily. 'No . . . third? . . . second . . .' Then with a mighty roar he leapt from his seat. Lillian had won, nailing Pollock on the line by half a stride. Coleman was shouting excitedly and the Los Angeles crowd was going mad. In the space of sixty yards she had cleaved through the best in the world as if they were second rate club runners. Judy Pollock summed up the amazement. 'Lillian,' she gasped, seconds after they had gone through the tape, 'I never thought it would be you.'

Lillian was numb. Everywhere people were shouting and cameras were flashing, but she couldn't take it in. Arthur Gold, secretary of the A.A.A. sat in the stand blinking back tears of joy. The loudspeaker announcement broke through Lillian's trance. 'First, Lillian Board for the Commonwealth in 52·8 . . . one of the most remarkable upsets in the history of women's track and field.'

She fell weeping into the arms of Marea Hartman, the British team manager. 'If only daddy could have been here,' she sobbed. 'If only daddy could have been here.'

EUROPE, CANADA, MEXICO AND CUBA

Overnight Lillian was transformed from potential world beater to world beater . . . from a well-known athlete to a national celebrity. Her blonde good looks smiled from every national newspaper to educate the millions who might have missed the race on T.V. And the stories of her fabulous future carried, as George described, 'the biggest headlines since war broke out.'

Mary Rand had also won in Los Angeles with a leap of 21 ft 2 in in the long jump. But already Lillian was heralded as the new 'Golden Girl' and, as journalists searched further for clichés, 'Princess of Pace', 'Golden Goddess' and 'Queen of the Quarter'. Her Los Angeles time of 52·8 was second only to Ann Packer in the European all-time list and people were not slow to spot this as more than co-incidence. Could Lillian, as Ann had so narrowly failed to do in Tokyo, win gold in both the 400 and 800 at the Mexico Olympics the following year?

Bob Trevor of the London *Evening News* was quickly off the mark. He wrote the day after Lillian's success in Los Angeles: 'Her break-through last night came on the same track where the late Tommy Hampson took the Olympic 800 metres crown for Britain in 1932. Here may be a significant parallel. For Miss Board clearly has the makings of the greatest two-lap runner the world of women's sport has seen. She is the athlete to defend Ann Packer's title for us in the Mexico Olympics.'

What was the reason for Lillian's amazing breakthrough?

Lillian, with her usual brand of sincere modesty, endeared herself to millions by saying only, 'I was so scared of coming last it spurred me on.' George, though, had the real answer. The day before Lillian had left for America he had taken her to Alperton for a session of differentials. That is trying to run the second half of a quarter faster than the first. They had arrived at the track to find the groundsmen working on it with sprinklers. But the men had cleared away their equipment especially so Lillian could train.

The differentials had gone well. George had told Lillian to cover the first 220 in about 30 seconds and the second 220 in 28 seconds. 'I want you to go out fast from the blocks for about ninety yards,' he told her. 'Then keep a fast stride down the back straight. At the 220 mark push harder and when you get to within sixty yards of the tape give it all you've got.' She had run three of these with five minutes recovery between each. In Los Angeles she had simply run a fourth and the stimulus of competition and occasion had brought the vast improvement in time.

Even at this stage, though, some people were not prepared to give George the credit due to him. Knowing little of Lillian's background, they looked on George as an interfering father who would be better advised to hand his daughter over to a professional coach. By now he was content to accept the criticism with a resigned annoyance at the injustice of it all.

Others, though, did appreciate the role he had played, and one was Robbie Brightwell, captain of the British team at the Tokyo Olympics. He wrote to George at the time of Los Angeles; 'Certainly your support and interest have greatly encouraged your daughter in her recent rise to fame—a step that will be followed by even greater recognition in the years to come.'

Lillian had little time to bask in her newly-won fame before she set off on a barnstorming tour of Europe. By the start of August she had landed a string of victories that had her fans looking towards the Mexican sunshine with gold-tinted glasses. The list read: July 17th, European Cup semi-final (Oslo), 1st 400 m (53·8); July 29th, Hungary v Great

Britain (Budapest), 1st 400 m (54·1); August 2nd, Poland v Great Britain (Szczecin), 1st 400 m (54·3). And between this she had found time to lower her personal best for the 220 to 24·6 at Guildford, Surrey, on July 22nd.

The irregularity of the life was catching up, though, as Lillian found on August 9th when she flew to Montreal to represent Europe against the Americas. For the past three weeks she had been living out of suitcases, unable to train properly and gradually becoming more and more stale mentally. She finished third behind Sweden's Karen Walgren, who won in 53·7. Lillian's time of 54·6 was still ·4 inside the Olympic qualifying time.

Lillian returned home wearily but worldly-wise. She still retained traces of her earlier naivety although much of it was replaced by a new-found sophistication. George and Frances were a little anxious that her new jet-set life might give her ideas of leaving home. Lillian quashed their fears without any prompting when she turned one night on her way to bed to tell them 'You know, even after seeing half the world, I wouldn't want to change anything about this house. This is where I belong.'

After three weeks at home Lillian left for Font Remeu in the Pyrenees for altitude training in preparation for the Mexico Olympics. 'It seems a bit daft going all that way to work out the correct training methods,' George told Frances. 'I would have thought it was obvious that if you've got to learn to combat lack of oxygen you simply have to lower your recovery time between each training repetition. That way you create your own oxygen debt and learn to overcome it.'

George's 'commonsense' turned out to be right. Lillian was advised to use repetition training and cut down on recovery times. Denis Watts wrote to George telling him of the findings and added. 'After this period at altitude I am more than ever convinced that Lillian is the greatest athlete I have had the fortune to be associated with during my career.' George was naturally pleased by the praise although Denis wasn't telling him anything he didn't know already! More important, though, was the fact that the way he had been training Lillian had now been proved the best possible preparation for Mexico.

From Font Remeu Lillian travelled to Kiev, Russia, and the final of the European Cup. Her altitude training showed its benefit as she sped to Britain's only gold of the meeting with 53·7 in the 400 metres. A week later she was at the White City winning a 400 against West Germany in 53·5. It was a fine run, but George could sense her fatigue as they left the stadium that evening. 'That's the finish of this season, thank goodness,' he said. 'You deserve a good, long rest. Six wins in seven internationals, it's a wonderful record.'

A sudden phone call from the British Amateur Athletic Board ended Lillian's hopes of a break. They wanted her to compete in the Little Olympics in Mexico City on October 15th–16th. Lillian reluctantly agreed and arrived in Mexico City to find that the other 400 metre girls had been resting and building up specially for that race. A jaded Lillian finished fifth in the final in 54·0 to America's Charlotte Cooke, who won in 52·8. 'I feel completely shattered,' Lillian said afterwards. 'It's been a tremendously tough season. I've been away from home on and off for almost a solid three months. I just want to get back and settle down into a routine again.' On the way back to England she tapped her last dregs of stamina to honour an invitation in Havana, Cuba, and win a 400 in 54·9.

And still the Mexico build-up went on. The British public had been given its four-yearly reminder that there was another sport besides football, shaken off its usual apathy over athletics and become caught in a huge wave of enthusiasm, so intense it was almost a remorseful apology for previous lack of interest. Lillian was caught in the middle of it. As one of Britain's brightest gold medal hopes she was the target of almost every sportswriter, feature writer and photographer in Fleet Street and its surrounds. She was photographed walking, talking, running, laughing; frontways, sideways, sitting, standing, looking happy, looking serious, looking blank . . . blank 'Whoops, sorry, forgot the film. Can we just do it again, please? . . . sorry about that.' And so it went on. Hour after hour, night after night.

57

Rain or shine, sleet or snow. Lillian lent her life to the one-eyed newscaster of Fleet Street.

She was recognised in the street, spoken to in restaurants, congratulated by fans, insulted by cranks wherever she went. She was fêted like a pop idol, a film star. She characterised all that was good in modern youth, said one paper. She should be considered as a lady-in-waiting for the Queen, said another. Her views were sought, and readily, articulately given on subjects ranging from sliced bread to the space programme . . .

ON MONEY: I like the good things in life—but only as a bonus. I can't begin to understand why some girls marry for money. If I was really in love with somebody I'd be quite happy living in one room with a couple of boxes to sit on.

ON RELIGION: I believe in God and still say my prayers every night although I don't feel the need to go to church. I feel so ruthless in competition that I sometimes worry that perhaps I'm not good enough to go to Heaven, if there is such a place.

ON SPORTSWOMEN: In Britain we are regarded as something of a freak, members of the butch set. But sport is as natural as eating or sleeping. You've only got to look at the British athletics team to see that the girls have all got lovely figures. In fact Britain is the only country where physical effort is looked on as something a little strange. I was so conscious of this when I first started road training that I used to carry a letter in my hand and pretend I was running for the post. In any other country you can run round without getting a second glance, let alone the usual comments like, 'Knees up . . .'

ON MARRIAGE: I think it is a wonderful institution and I want to get married and have about three children. But that doesn't mean that I wouldn't live with someone if I loved him and for one reason or other we couldn't get married.

Along with the Press, television and radio came the invitations. Lillian was asked to open fêtes, speak at prize-givings, kick-off soccer matches and attend a whole string of dinner-dances. She had entered a whole new world which was poles apart from the lonely hours she had spent pounding round damp cinder tracks. And, with her ability to give of her best in good-class company, she thrived on the glitter and glamour without ever losing her basic modesty or little-girl charm.

Like so many other people who excel at a sport, Lillian had always had a limited knowledge about other athletic personalities. Her concentration was focused too fully on her own progress and ambitions and the form of a few respected rivals to take in the broader aspects of the sport. Tony Duffy, a freelance sports photographer and close friend of Lillian and her family, recalls the time some people were enthusing over the sprinting of American Olympic gold medallist Jim Hines. Lillian, coming in at the tail-end of the conversation, shattered everybody with a bland, 'Jim Hines, who's he?' With her entrance to the social merry-go-round Lillian's knowledge of names and faces grew. But Tony always sensed it was more from fear of appearing insular than from genuine interest.

Lillian by now had no lack of potential boy-friends. She went out with a few to official functions but otherwise preferred the company of Trevor Wells, a family friend of Mary Rand and her Olympic oarsman husband, Sidney. Trevor, part owner of a family printing business, had been introduced to Lillian shortly before her trip to Los Angeles while she was spending one of her frequent weekends at Mary's house near Henley. They went steady for a year and a half and there was talk of an engagement at one time. But each had too strong a pull to their chosen careers— Trevor in building up his business and Lillian in her athletics—and eventually they drifted apart although always remaining friends.

Apart from Trevor and the friends she had made while still a young girl, Lillian now found herself in the sophisticated social climate of knowing hundreds of people . . .

briefly. She had little opportunity to make friends among fellow athletes because of the jealousy bred by success and off the track she was wary of hangers-on and name-droppers who would find reflected glory from a shallow relationship with her. The result was that Lillian Board, one of the best known and best liked sports personalities in the country, was almost a lonely figure amid the hurly-burly of a social life that would have graced any debutante. Almost—because she had her family. And she began to find that it was only in the cosy security of her own house that she could really relax and be what she always considered herself—an ordinary girl who happened to have a talent for athletics. Certainly, she had worked hard to build on that talent, but she had done it purely for self-satisfaction, not in search of fame.

Her complex feelings were best described by herself when she said, 'It's almost as if I've got a split personality. I miss the limelight a little when I'm not in it. But as soon as people start crowding round for interviews, photographs and autographs I often feel it would be nice to be just ordinary and do what I want, say what I want without causing comment.'

Writer Helen Speed, interviewing Lillian for the magazine *Woman*, was quick to spot Lillian's knack of self-analysis. She wrote: 'She is remarkably perceptive about herself, perhaps because she has time for reflection, living the loneliness that being a runner imposes.'

Patrick Canty in the *Daily Mirror* Magazine called it 'almost cynical self-awareness' and went on to give perhaps one of the best pen pictures of Lillian:

She is the supergirl next door; the girl any son could bring home in the knowledge that she would say all the right things to mum and make dad feel twenty years younger.

And she's such a nice girl that people identify easily with her. Her triumphs and failures become intensely personal issues to people across the country. That long-legged blonde lisping shy, composed comments to a television commentator after the race, isn't Lillian Board at all. It's everyone's daughter or girl friend. And she's a credit to them.

But there is more to her than that. For while she is certainly a nice girl—a description, incidentally, which would horrify her—the eternal composure hints at an inbred shrewdness.

Nice but shrewd, shy but confident, competitive but compassionate. Lillian was all these things and she came to understand herself during the solitary hours of training, the loneliness of crowded receptions and the restful solitude of her bedroom which was her castle.

Lillian's family by now had geared almost their whole lives to athletics. The household revolved around her training timetable and fixture list. Mealtimes, appointments, outings and holidays were arranged with one eye on the clock and the other on the calendar. And, like Lillian, Frances, Irene and the two Georges suddenly found their company was sought by people who had previously passed them by.

Irene, as the twin, was the natural target for would-be gossips. 'But surely you're jealous, aren't you? Oh, c'mon, you can tell me. All those nice places, meeting all those people, pictures in the paper. You must be jealous. You wouldn't be human if you weren't.' At first Irene tried to explain that jealousy had never crossed her mind; that if Lillian was at last getting some perks from athletics it was only because of years and years of hard slog—and more in the future; that all she felt about Lillian's achievements was deep admiration and a wholehearted wish that she went on to fulfil her ambitions.

Gradually, though, she realised that this kind of attitude was hardly the material her questioners wanted to hear for their High Street chatter. She could read in their eyes that they chose not to believe a word she was saying and eventually she stopped trying to explain her feelings and her frustration when people came up to her at work with, 'Excuse me Lillian . . . oh, I'm sorry, I mean Irene.'

61

Or stopped her in the street with, 'Hello, Irene, how's Lillian?'

'They do it simply to show that they have a connection with Lillian through me,' Irene told her mother. 'They're not in the least bit genuine.'

Irene's true friends never needed to ask her if she was jealous. Her irritability before a big race was evidence enough of her wanting Lillian to win; and her joy when she did was almost as great as Lillian's. In this way Irene was probably Lillian's most unselfish fan. She was disgusted by reflected glory and so stood only to lose all the time Lillian was winning. But above almost everything else she wanted Lillian to win. 'I just want Lillian to be happy,' she would say. 'I know it sounds corny, but it's true.' And it was.

Irene's brother found other pressures. He felt he had a duty to Lillian to maintain her shining image and so went out of his way to make sure that every piece of work he did in the building trade was done as quickly and as well as possible. And there were sacrifices. Frances was almost a track-widow with George away almost every evening. Lillian was the first to recognise this, 'People talk about sacrifices,' she said once. 'But I'm not really giving up anything. I'm doing athletics because I want to. I think mummy makes the biggest sacrifice because my training takes up so much of my father's time.'

Irene, too, was aware of her mother being left alone and would often give up the chance of going out to stay in and keep her company. On race days it was the same, with Irene and Frances sitting in the stand while George stood at the trackside giving Lillian last minute instructions. But Lillian always knew where her mother and sister were as soon as the race started. 'It doesn't matter how much noise is going on,' she said, 'I can always pick out your two voices shouting me on.'

OLYMPIC GAMES IN MEXICO

Lillian started her winter training on December 28th with the boost of being nominated Athlete of the Year by the Athletic Writers' Association. She built up even more stamina with increased weight training and road running and began sharpening her speed in mid-January with regular trips to Crystal Palace's tartan track. Lillian, unlike many other athletes, enjoyed running on tartan, especially in winter when cinder tracks tended to be slippery and dangerous. She was inspired, also, by the atmosphere at the Palace and liked the friendly helpfulness of Emlyn Jones, the stadium director. George took his cine-camera along for most of these sessions and played back the film in slow motion as soon as it was developed the same evening so they could analyse and correct any faults in Lillian's action.

At the end of March Lillian was invited to attend a training course in Cork, Ireland. George refused to let her go. He had two reasons: first, he did not want to break her regular routine, and second he felt that as far as Lillian was concerned the special courses did more harm than good. His feelings went back to 1966 when Lillian had attended a course at Morecambe. While she was warming up one of the coaches had called her over.

'You've got to put more effort into it,' he told her.

'I'm only warming up,' Lillian answered in amazement.

'O.K.' he said, 'but you must always be determined to give it everything when you're racing.'

'I always do,' she told him.

Immediately after this course Lillian had gone to another in the Midlands. After watching her run the coach called her over, 'You've got to learn to relax, we have enough blood and thunder rugby-type runners.' Lillian had returned home with her head spinning. She told George, 'I've met most of the top coaches in the country now . . . and I'll settle for you.'

It was this conflict of opinion which had made George turn down the chance of taking a senior coaching examination. He had told Lillian. 'I'm not having them mark my card. As far as you're concerned I know best. Our partnership started when you were a baby. You were the heavier twin so I always had to carry you around; your mother looked after Irene. I've watched you grow up. I know your temperament, your whole character inside out . . . and for the past seven years we've had a date every night, more than most courting couples. Our minds are in tune completely. It's you and I against the world and nobody's going to come between us.'

By the spring of 1968, with Lillian's Olympic build-up in full swing, George had lost patience with well-meaning advice from men he felt were less qualified than he to coach Lillian.

At about the same time George became disenamoured with the Press, Lillian had always been praised in almost embarrassingly glowing terms in the papers, but the constant flow of telephone calls and evening photograph sessions had worn George down. 'Most of the reporters are grand lads to stand around and drink with,' he told Lillian. 'But once some of them get behind a typewriter they get power complexes, telling you what you should and shouldn't do. And as for some of those photographers, they're just parasites. They make money out of us, but don't even give us a set of prints in return. It's all grab, grab, grab.'

Nor would George be swayed by arguments that it was because of the Press that Lillian had become a national celebrity. 'Lillian's not a film star,' he said. 'She doesn't need her name in the paper to get a job. If she keeps on winning they'll have to write about her. They're not doing us any favours, they're just a bloody nuisance half of them. It wouldn't be so bad if they all knew something about athletics, but some of them ask such stupid, inane questions that you want to scream.'

George's strong views about the Press were motivated mainly by a feeling of injustice. He felt it was wrong that sportswriters could put forward their views on Lillian and perhaps be read by millions whereas his own views, which he naturally felt were the right ones, were only rarely printed. Also, he was annoyed that Lillian and he could spend hours with a photographer for little more than a thank you. He had similar treatment from the B.B.C. A camera-crew spent three days shooting an episode on Lillian for a programme and then, besides failing to send even a letter of thanks, neglected to tell them when the programme would be shown. With the pressures of Mexico all around him George did not have the time or inclination to find excuses for that sort of behaviour. T.V. and the Press were *Them*; Lillian and he were *Us*.

Lillian by now was working in Ealing Town Hall as a typist. She had been posted there by her temporary agency, been offered a permanent job, and taken it. George was a little worried that the strain of holding down a regular job plus the necessary increase in training might prove too much. He was searching for an answer when it dropped into his lap. Ted Hart, a ghost-writer who carried the nick-name of the Angel of Fleet Street, asked if he could employ Lillian as a home typist. 'I won't want her to do very much, so it will give her plenty of time for training,' he told George.

George searched for the catch. But there was none. Ted was a genuine athletics fan who wanted to help Lillian. He had a sketchy idea that he wanted to start a freelance agency with a big name in sport writing for him. But that was a long way in the future and he told George, 'It may not even come about, but if it does all I want is first refusal of Lillian's name for athletics articles.' After a couple of meetings with Ted, George knew he liked and trusted him. Lillian duly left the Town Hall, and because, as Ted had promised, the work was negligible found she could devote herself almost entirely to athletics.

And she did. She was to tell Irene a year later, 'All that spring and summer the only thing that was important to me was winning a gold medal. I used to go to bed and dream about being on the rostrum. I would wake up and the first thing I'd think about was drinking the victory champagne. Nothing else mattered. It seems wrong now that I could be so wrapped up in it. But I was, completely.'

So were the public. The Olympic flame had been lit in their minds and they were hungry for information. The papers and magazines were quick to provide it. Neil Allen, writing in *World Sports*, gave as good an insight into Lillian's character as any at that time. 'This young girl from Ealing has the mind of a champion. She is ambitious and yet cautious. She dreams big dreams and yet she is realistic. She sets out to run the opposition into the ground and yet she is genuinely modest. She is thrilled by victory and yet she learns from defeat . . . Lillian has a very good chance of winning a medal.'

Allen's considered view that Lillian 'has a very good chance of winning a medal' was shared by most of the thinking Press. A couple, though, went overboard with firm declarations that Lillian was a gold medal certainty. 'Honestly,' Lillian complained, 'you'd think they were staging this race just for me. They say to me "Who do you think your biggest rival is?" as if the gold was already mine and I was picking out the silver and bronze medallists.'

Other sportswriters, harping back to Bob Trevor's Los Angeles theme, suggested Lillian should tackle both the 400 and 800 in Mexico as Ann Packer had done at Tokyo. George bore with the speculation for a while, then ended it with one swift statement: 'Ann was twenty-two at Tokyo, Lillian's nineteen. These games are at altitude and people are already saying that running there could be harmful. No flesh or blood of mine is going to kill herself for the sake of a medal. Her chance at the 800 will come . . . when she's matured.'

Lillian emerged from her winter training programme—three sessions a week of weights, two of stamina track work and two of speed sharpening—stronger, faster and fitter than ever. She stood 5 ft 6 in. and weighed 9 st 8 lb. Her improvement in speed was spectacular. Her best 220 yard time in 1967 was 24·6 with 24·3 in a time trial, yet on June 1st she won the Southern title in 23·7 after a tremendous race with Della James that revived memories of their duels as intermediates. It was as marked an improvement as George had dared hope for. It meant Lillian could now handle the first 200 of a 400 in 24·5—and still have a bit in hand. That was the kind of pace that would be necessary in Mexico.

A week later Lillian made her season's 440 debut at an inter-club meeting in Brighton. The stresses of being a top Olympic hope were highlighted. For, instead of the quiet, almost private test she had wanted, she found herself surrounded by T.V. cameras and Press-men. And, as she walked to the start, the announcer blithely reeled off the world, European and British records for the distance! She won with 54·8, comfortably inside the Olympic qualifying time; a really sound opener, but it provoked headlines like 'Lillian fails'.

Three days later at Reading Lillian tried her first 880 of the season and sprinted home easily with a powerful last 220. Her time of 2 min 7 sec was just two-tenths outside the Olympic qualifying standard and she had a three and a half second lead over the next girl home, Sheila Taylor (now Carey). But again some people saw it as a disappointing performance. This reaction to a minor race was, in itself, insignificant. Its importance grew in the next few days, though, through a chain of events which proved it was George and not Denis Watts who had control of Lillian.

A group of pressmen, discussing Lillian's 880 with Denis two days later, asked him what had gone wrong. Denis did not know the result or times of the race and, perhaps fearing that Lillian had flopped disastrously and that he would be held responsible, told the reporters he had not been in touch with George recently and knew nothing about Lillian's form. The result was a spate of telephone calls to George asking him, 'Who really is coaching Lillian?' George tactfully refused to add to Denis's embarrassment. He told the callers merely what they had been told before: that Denis handled the broader aspects of Lillian's training while he was the man on the spot who noted the progress. A couple of the papers, baulked in what could have been a controversial story, then chose to go the other way. John Reed in the *Sunday Express* wrote under the heading 'Who is coaching Britain's top woman athlete?': '. . . as good a job as George Board has done with Lillian she should be in the hands of a professional.' The timing could hardly have been worse. For in the bottom corner of the same page a smaller headline proclaimed 'Lillian beats the world' and went on to describe a 53·5 400 metre victory she had notched up in Moscow the previous night.

Lillian, encouraged tremendously by her Moscow run, which put her at the head of the world rankings for the season, returned to London to show once again that she now had the edge over Della James. Despite the fact that her training was geared to 400 and 800 metres, Lillian scorched through a gusty head wind to win the London Olympiades 200 metre club title in 24·3 with Della and Mary Rand trailing in second and third with 25·0. A 10·9 100 yards victory over international Madeleine Cobb the following week completed George's early season preparations. Lillian was now the best 200 metre sprinter in Britain and the fastest 400 metre runner in the world. And she was still building her stamina for future 800s.

Lillian and George showed their dislike of soft victories and empty titles with the coming of the Women's A.A.A. championships. Lillian, knowing she could walk away with the 400 metre title, chose instead to have a dabble in the 800 against Vera Nikolic, the European champion and favourite for the Olympic 800 metres gold. George explained his reasons to the Press with, 'There's no room at the top for those with a negative attitude and weak character. You've got to be courageous.'

Lillian lowered her personal best to win her heat in 2 min 5·7 sec on Friday, July 19th. In the final the following day Nikolic broke the world record with 2:00·5 while Lillian gave an exciting insight into her depths of almost untapped talent by taking second place in 2:02·0.

'Actually, it's a bit shattering to run your fastest-ever time and still get beaten,' Lillian said afterwards. 'I felt ten years older after than run. I'm far happier in my mind knowing I'm not doing the 800 as well as the 400 in Mexico. It sounds very good, second to Ann Packer and all that, but I just don't have the experience over 800.'

Nikolic's reaction to her victory showed once again the kind of attitude Lillian's success engendered in her rivals. 'I just had to win the race,' she said. 'I was jealous of Lillian. She was the centre of attraction for journalists in London all the time. They always asked her to make statements and ignored me.' Lillian, by now a veteran at dealing with that kind of statement, answered coolly, 'I'm sorry Vera felt like that. But I must say I find it all rather amusing. Naturally, being a British girl the British journalists wanted to boost me up. I didn't feel her resentment at all. We got on very well together and she certainly didn't indicate in any way that she was jealous of me.'

Back trouble, which was to plague Lillian over the next two years, started in early August. But it did not stop her running what George and many others felt was the finest sprint of her career—a 23·5 200 metres in the wind-swept Great Britain versus West Germany match at the White City on August 3rd. Only Dorothy Hyman with 23·2 had ever run faster for Britain—and Lillian's performance had come on a track so devoid of life it was known as the 'Graveyard of Champions'.

The pain in Lillian's back grew worse and started to spread to her legs and ankles. Alf Cotton and Mary Rand suggested she visited Ron Ettridge, a blind physiotherapist who lived at Addiscombe, near Croydon, Surrey. He diagnosed strained ligaments in the vertebrae and began treating her three times a week. It was an hour and a half bus journey for Lillian, but she enjoyed making the trip. She got on well with Ron and his wife and they, in turn, treated her almost like one of the family.

During Lillian's first visit to Addiscombe Ron insisted that she took George along next time so he could see for himself the kind of man who was treating his daughter. Then he gave Lillian an impromptu demonstration of his skill. He ran his fingers over her legs and announced, 'I should say you have a stride length of about 7 ft 6 in.' His perfect estimation gave Lillian increased confidence; and as she grew to know him so her admiration deepened for the philosophical way he treated his blindness and used it almost as a tool to help his sense of touch. After a few visits, Lillian's legs and ankles responded to the treatment, but she was still troubled by her back. Complete rest would have been the best answer, but with the Olympics approaching that was out of the question. Instead, Ron and George modified Lillian's training schedule so she could maintain her fitness with the minimum of strain on her back.

With her back supported by a plaster measuring 9″ by 9″, she ran her last 400 metres before leaving for Mexico in an international against Poland at the White City on September 2nd. She won comfortably in 53 seconds, having clocked 24·8 at the 200 mark. The same afternoon in the 4 × 100 metre relay Lillian took over the baton on the last leg two yards ahead of Irena Szewinska (nee Kertzenstein), the world record holder for the 100 and 200 metres. Nobody gave Lillian a chance, but she overcame the handicap of her injury to hold off the legendary Polish girl by a tenth of a second for an overall time of 44·6.

Lillian's sprinting was now at its peak and, watching her, George felt a twinge of sympathy for the other British girl sprinters. It must be soul-destroying for them, he thought, to see Lillian winning over the shorter distances in what were really only training runs for the 400, while they were trying their hardest merely to reach Olympic qualifying times. Her superiority was displayed at its most devastating at Portsmouth on Saturday, September 14th, in a Great

Britain versus The Rest match—the Olympic squad's last appearance in Britain before they left for Mexico. She powered home in the 200 with 23·6 leaving the other girls almost embarrassingly stranded. Della James was second with 24·4, Janet Simpson third (24·4), Madeleine Cobb fourth (24·5) and Penny Pawsey fifth (25·0).

In the 4 × 110 yards relay Lillian ended for all time any argument over her comparison with Della. Taking over the baton just in front of Della, who was running for The Rest, Lillian pulled away dramatically to help Britain to a world record of 45 seconds and prompt Della's father to come over to George and tell him, 'Congratulations. I always thought Della had the edge on Lillian, but today has proved me wrong.' It was just the combination to send Lillian off to Mexico in high spirits.

George had had booked to go to Mexico with a party from the magazine *Athletics Weekly*, which was leaving London on October 11th, just after the Games had started. Frances and Irene decided to stay home for fear the tension would be too much. In the three weeks before he flew out, after Lillian had gone, George felt lost. 'I'm like a fish out of water,' he told his friends in the 'Myllet'. 'My routine's been completely destroyed.'

He was also worried about the reports of student riots in Mexico City, only a few miles from the Olympic Village. The athletes seemed to be in no danger, but there was talk of cancelling the Olympics unless the situation eased. He scoured every national paper for details and waited impatiently for Lillian's letters. They arrived regularly and gradually put his mind at rest. She sounded perfectly happy and relaxed and her training was going exceptionally well. She had been entered for the 200 and 4 × 100 metre relay as well as the 400 and in time trials had clocked 23·2 for the 200 and an outstanding 36·3 for 300 metres—equivalent in pace to 48·4 for the 400.

George was a little perturbed that Lillian had been entered in three events. He would have preferred her to have been allowed to concentrate on the 400.

In Mexico George was met at the airport by Lillian and

Marea Hartman, the British women's team manager. Lillian quickly brought George up-to-date with an almost ceaseless flow of gay chatter that fully justified T.V. commentator David Coleman's description, 'If there's one thing you can do better than run, Lillian, it's talk.'

Lillian's first 400 metre heat was scheduled for Monday, October 14th, and as he sat in his hotel over the weekend, George could feel the tension building up inside him. By the Monday he was off his food and exhausted after an almost sleepless night. The fourteen-mile taxi ride to the stadium had become a daily nightmare. The driving was atrocious with cars careering across the roads without a semblance of order and the constant din of angry horns. 'It's a miracle we ever get there,' George told his friends at the hotel. 'It's worse than anything the Keystone Cops ever dreamt of.'

The atmosphere of the stadium, though, made every minute of the journey worth while. As he took his place in the stand on that Monday afternoon George imagined himself in the role of Sir Matt Busby or Don Revie watching Manchester United or Leeds in the F.A. Cup Final at Wembley. The preparations were over, the seemingly endless discussions had ended; now Lillian was on her own. George watched her strolling towards the start with growing anxiety. The hip flask he had filled only that morning was already feeling ominously light. 'Of course she'll qualify,' he told himself. 'It will be easy. So why are you worrying?' But he was past logic. The report of the starting pistol made him jump, although he had been expecting it, and it was not until the girls had covered the first 200 that he felt himself relaxing. Lillian hit the straight a couple of feet behind Cuba's Aurelia Penton with the others strung out well behind. The Cuban went on to win in 52·8 and then promptly collapsed while Lillian came through a tenth slower but still looking strong.

George stayed to watch the other two British 400 metre entries, Janet Simpson and Mary Green qualify for the next round. But his mind was elsewhere. He had to get into the athletes' quarters to contact Lillian, but he had no official pass. Suddenly he remembered he had Lillian's Mexico issue peaked cap in his pocket. She had refused to wear it, preferring a more feminine pink hat she had found in a local boutique. But for George it was the obvious answer.

He made his way to the Olympic village with Charlie Swainston, a P.E. teacher from South Shields who had befriended him at the hotel. Then, squaring his cap firmly on his head, he mingled with the athletes, gesticulated at a distant figure with his programme and marched past the police at the check point. Knowing Lillian's appetite, George decided his best bet was to wait outside the dining room. And, sure enough, after about ten minutes she turned up. They found a table together in the huge canteen and George at last had the chance to ask his questions. 'How did you feel afterwards,' he probed. 'Were you all in?'

'Really, Daddy,' Lillian answered almost with disdain. 'Surely you could see I was well within myself.' George felt like a small boy who had spoken out of turn, but took the ticking off happily.

'That's tremendous,' he said. 'But in the semi-final tomorrow you'd better be prepared to put a bit more into the final sprint. You were in the fastest race today and it may be the same tomorrow. We don't want you caught on the line.'

George made arrangements to meet Lillian the following evening and turned to leave. 'Good God,' he said, looking round at the other athletes. 'I thought you ate a lot, but look at some of these. If their plates fell backwards they'd be buried.'

A thunderstorm more intense than anything George had seen before was raging as he set off for the stadium the next afternoon along with Charlie Swainston and two other new-found friends, Les Rigg, a turf accountant from Barrow-in-Furness, and his wife, Muriel. The taxi ride was the worst yet. Visibility was almost zero but the driver hurtled through the streets as if they were Liverpool High Street at 3.5 p.m. on Cup Final day. They arrived at the stadium with a few moments to spare before Lillian's race. George leapt from the taxi, leaving the others to carry out the customary bartering over fare prices, and charged towards the entrance. The rain hit him as if he had walked into a fireman's hose. Someone called after him, 'You can't go across there in that.'

'Look, mate,' he shouted back, 'I was born in Manchester. And you don't think I could go back home and tell Frances I missed the semi-final because of a bit of bloody rain, do you?'

The vast stadium was almost deserted and the flags hung limply from their masts as George burst out of the tunnel. He flung himself into the nearest seat and stamped his feet, watching the water squirt through the lace-holes of his shoes. He had arrived just in time to see Janet Simpson go through to the final with 54·0 for third place in the first semi-final. In front of her were Helga Henning (West Germany, 53·3) and Colette Besson (France, 53·6). Aurelia Penton of Cuba was fourth with 54·0.

The rain seemed to stop almost abruptly as the girls hit the tape and George could make out Lillian's figure at the track-side. As usual, she was playing with her hair and fiddling with her shorts—mannerisms she used even before training sessions but which some people had wrongly diagnosed as acute nervousness. She had drawn lane six which had managed to stay in reasonable condition apart from the occasional puddle. George gave silent thanks that Lillian had never minded wet, windy conditions, due partly to her fighting character and partly to his style of training.

Lillian got off to a good start and, carrying out George's instructions, hit a fast pace down the back straight while still keeping some in hand for the finish. She reached the final turn four yards behind the leading girl with three others bunched around her. Then, with fluid ease, she increased her pace and cleaved through to win in a personal best 52·5. Behind her came Van Der Hoeven (Holland, 52·6), Natalia Pechenkina (Russia, 52·8) and Jarvis Scott (U.S.A., 53·2). Mary Green was fifth and eliminated with a personal best 53·6, a time which would have been easily enough in the first semi-final. Again Lillian told George she had a bit in hand. 'It felt such an easy run that I was surprised the time was so good. I know I can do better in tomorrow's final.'

Lillian was a firm favourite for the gold, quoted at 3 to 1 by trackside bookmakers. But by now she was used to the pressures and ballyhoo. Tucked away in the comparative privacy of the Olympic village and surrounded by hundreds of athletes who had been through the same publicity mangle in their own countries, she was as happy and relaxed as she had ever been before a major race. She had worked and waited for this race. Tomorrow everything would be condensed into an all-out effort lasting considerably less than a minute. It was the magic minute that had ruled her life completely for the past two years. Now the waiting was nearly over; her chance to do something about her biggest ambition was a few hours away and she looked forward to it eagerly.

Back in Ealing, though, the atmosphere was taut. Irene was in bed with an upset stomach, the result of nervous tension. In three weeks her weight had dropped by half a stone. Frances, too, was finding it hard to maintain her usual composure and spent a sleepless night on the eve of the final. Their feelings were shared to a lesser extent throughout the country among Lillian's growing number of admirers. And most of them, unlike Frances and Irene, had Lillian down as a certainty to follow David Hemery on the gold-medal rostrum.

Their views were echoed by Bob Trevor in the *Evening News*. On the day of the final he wrote, 'Next it is Lillian Board's turn to win gold . . . in the 400 metres final tonight. I see only the Dutch girl Hermine Van Der Hoeven and America's Jarvis Scott as potential rivals. But let's forget them: It's Lillian to win. The British team has ordered more champagne . . . and I say they are right.' And indeed, the British team had ordered more champagne. It sat cooling in ice like a tempter of fate as Lillian peeled off her track-suit for the final. There was champagne, too, in living rooms all over Britain as people prepared their victory toasts. And there was champagne in the offices of the London *Daily Mail* where Princess Margaret had accepted an invitation to watch the race in the editorial department. The Princess had sent a Good Luck message to Lillian before the final.

From a royal viewer down to the unemployed who clustered round a T.V. in the public bar of an East End pub, all eyes were on Lillian. But none were more intense than George's as he sat cooped up in a T.V. control room overlooking the stadium, wondering why he had ever agreed to go on the air a few minutes before the race. He had spent the whole afternoon sitting quietly as commentators Adrian Metcalfe and Lionel Pugh gave a non-stop account of the events. Chris Chataway sat next to him. He dearly wished to be with his hotel friends, but the T.V. crew were frightened of losing him in the crowds.

As he sat there fidgeting and counting away the minutes George mulled over the draw. Lillian was in lane one and he wasn't happy about it. He had three reasons: First, athletes tended to run wide if they were up against the kerb of the track for fear of tripping themselves. Second, in an eight-lane Olympic final the stagger between the first and eighth lane was enormous. Lillian, he feared, might be pulled through the first 200 metres at too fast a speed if the girl in the outside lane was the type to go flat out from the blocks. Lillian would see a huge gap in front of her and possibly try and close it. Third, the bends were tighter on the inside lane and therefore harder to round at full speed. He was happy, though, about his tactics. He had told Lillian to go fast for the first 100 yards, then maintain a strong stride down the back straight, give it everything round the final bend so she would hit the last 100 with a clear lead and then let her stamina from 800 metres and her sprinting speed carry her through.

As the girls put their blocks in place Adrian Metcalfe beckoned George to the microphone. What did he think of Lillian's chances? 'She has never run better,' George told the watching millions. 'She is fit and happy. She is going out for gold and a world record.'

The start was delayed for twenty minutes while officials waited for the end of the pole vault. Lillian had taken off her track-suit in preparation and sat during the delay with it wrapped loosely around her, fiddling with her hair and squinting into the sun. George sat watching her with his palms clammy and his mouth dry. But among all the emotions flitting through him the strongest was pride. That was his flesh and blood out there on an Olympic track waiting for an Olympic final which she was favourite to win. The long, lonely winter nights of training were suddenly worthwhile a dozen times over.

At last they were ready to go. Lillian settled into her blocks and was then forced to stand up again as one of the officials complained that her back foot was not touching the track correctly. George leaned to one of the T.V. crew. 'Every girl in this race is wearing the same make of shoe and using stadium blocks. Why do they have to pick on Lillian?' In his mind he was sure the answer was that Lillian was in lane one and the officials, in their brown suits and trilby hats, were disinclined to make the long haul to the outer lanes. George's stomach, which ached with the strain, unknotted with the starter's gun. Now they were back in business; this was the big one and it was under way.

Lillian got away well, made up the stagger on the two girls immediately outside her within 100 yards and then settled into a fast stride. George was screaming encouragement, all decorum gone. In Ealing Frances and Irene were on their knees in front of the T.V., pounding the floor with their fists, their throats raw. Everything was going as George had planned. Lillian lengthened her stride round the final bend and came into the home straight with a three-yard lead. George was on his feet now, tears streaming down his face. She was going to do it . . . she was going to win.

Then, with sixty yards to go he noticed the virtually unknown French girl Colette Besson moving powerfully in lane three. More powerfully than Lillian, in fact, and . . . yes, she was catching her. The last fifteen yards to the tape seemed to last the length of a marathon to George as he realised with a horrifying numbness that Lillian was fading. Lillian and Colette hit the tape almost together, but the French girl had dipped at the perfect split second. Lillian, looking sideways at her conqueror was caught in a frozen fraction of disbelief by a hundred Press cameras.

It had been Los Angeles in reverse. Colette, the unknown, producing a performance that made nonsense of her previous form, Lillian, the favourite, caught on the line by a tremendous finishing spurt. Colette's time of 52·0 equalled the Olympic record. Lillian was given 52·1, a British record.

The girls had barely stopped running when the T.V. microphones were again passed to George. But those who had expected him to be disappointed were surprised. 'Lillian ran a tremendous race,' he said, 'I'm proud of her. At the age of 19, in her first Olympics, she's won a silver medal and broken the British record. Fantastic.'

Lillian, walking from the trackside, was conscious only of a strange emptiness. It was all over. She had missed the gold. But she'd run her fastest ever. Yet at the back of her mind there was the fear she might be labelled a flop; that she had let down Britain.

This worry was made even more acute as Peter Lorenzo stepped forward to interview her for T.V. 'I thought you told me you were fit,' he said. 'That's right, I did,' Lillian answered, holding back her tears. 'And I've just won an Olympic silver medal.' She was besieged by the Press in the tunnel leading to the changing rooms. Their predominant question, 'What went wrong?' 'Nothing went wrong,' she told them as calmly as possible. 'Colette just ran faster than me.'

American athlete Vince Reel was coming out of the changing rooms as Lillian, finally free from the inquisition, went in. He later wrote in a magazine, 'What do you say to an Olympic favourite who's just been beaten for the gold? But I needn't have worried. She said "Hi", then "Good Luck". Then I think she said "Damn".'

Frances and Irene, like George, were happy with the

result. 'I think my daughter was fantastic,' Frances told reporters. 'She ran a tremendous race.'

But two papers saw it differently. 'Champagne turns to flat beer,' said the *Evening News*. 'Oh dear! only a silver for Lillian Board,' cried the *Daily Mirror*. Pictures of Lillian staring dejectedly at her silver medal on the rostrum backed up the stories. Lillian was to say later, 'People think I was sulking on the rostrum because I'd missed the gold. But I wasn't. I was just dazed. But I was upset mainly by the fact that some people seemed to be labelling me a failure.'

George, oblivious to what was happening in England, met Lillian with a beaming smile the same evening after the race. She looked at him apprehensively. 'Are you terribly disappointed, Daddy?'

'Disappointed? Don't be so daft. I'm proud of you. Really proud.'

'Oh, I'm so glad,' she said, her face brightening. 'I was worried you'd be upset. I thought you'd be asking me what went wrong like the Press and Denis Watts did.' She reached into her track-suit pocket. 'This is for you,' she said, pinning the small silver medal replica on George's lapel.

George celebrated Lillian's run into the early hours of the morning with champagne and brandy, a drink he had been introduced to by Les Rigg, and music from the strolling minstrels who entertained in the hotels. George had immediately taken a liking to the song 'Guantana-mera' and during his stay in Mexico asked for it almost every night. He looked upon it as his and Lillian's signature tune.

George returned home two days before the Olympic party after watching Lillian come sixth in the 200 metre semi-final with 23·4 a personal best time, and help the British team to seventh place in the final of the relay in 43·7, a British record. With better baton changing they might have been among the medals. For, apart from the U.S.A. team which won in 42·8 the next six were within four-tenths of a second of each other.

Lillian, as usual, brought back a basketful of presents for Frances and Irene. But the reunion lost its glitter when she and George spotted the offending headlines among the family's Mexico scrap-book. George was blazing. 'Why can't they accentuate the positive instead of the negative? How can she have lost a gold medal when she never had one? Why can't they say she won a silver and praise her like they did Sheila Sherwood?'—silver medallist in the long jump in her *second* Olympics.

Lillian, too, was bitterly disappointed. In the last few days in Mexico she had recovered from her earlier dismay and was happy and content with the silver. Her running was still showing a marked improvement each season and a silver was an excellent stepping stone for the future. Now, glancing through the cuttings, all pleasure had gone. 'Ignore this talk, Lillian,' George told her. 'It's ridiculous. They seem to forget Besson is three years older than you; and also they've praised Janet Simpson for coming fourth in the 400—and it's her second Olympics.' But the damage had been done. Lillian again began to think that the whole country felt she had let them down.

It was a reaction which Irene had been afraid of the day before the final. In a letter to George she had written, 'Oh, I'm so scared! I've been smoking such a lot. I'm frightened that if Lillian doesn't do as well as everyone expects of her, the Press and public will call her a failure. I hope this isn't going to happen because I think it might hurt her. Please give her all our love and tell her whatever the result might be, we're very proud of her.'

As Irene had feared, Lillian was hurt by the criticism and never completely forgave the Press. 'I feel sorry for a few of the reporters,' she told George in a moment of anger. 'They have an inferiority complex. They love to mix with well-known people. They love to write about some sport in which they would have liked to excel. They love to set themselves up as self-appointed judges and juries.'

George made his feelings felt with the next reporter who came round for a story. 'What were Lillian's future plans,' he asked. 'I'm not so sure there's going to be any future,'

George told him. 'It's a tough job wearing a gold medal round your neck for four years—it starts to get a bit heavy near the end. We're wondering if it's worth flogging ourselves to death for another four years with the chance of being called a failure again.' George felt guilty afterwards at having given him a false story. He and Lillian had absolutely no intention of giving up athletics. George couldn't. It was his life. But he had felt the need to hit out.

He felt the need to hit out with something a bit stronger than words a few weeks later when Lillian returned home with a copy of Chris Brasher's book *A Diary of the XIXth Olympics*. Brasher, a former Olympic gold medallist who had become a columnist in the *Observer*, had given the book to Lillian with the inscription: 'To Lillian Board, hoping that she will keep on so that we can have the pleasure of watching her on the track for many more seasons—especially in Munich 1972.'

'That's very nice of him,' George said.

'Wait till you read what the gentleman has written inside,' Irene told him.

George found the first reference on page 71. Brasher had written:

Lillian will, I am sure, win a gold medal one day if only she goes on with her athletics. But I do hope that she realises that a close relative is not the best coach for any athlete—or perhaps it is her father who should realise this and hand over the care of Lillian's athletic career to those who really know what they are doing. There is so much more to winning an Olympic title than just running.

Sixteen pages later Brasher added:

I am absolutely convinced that if Lillian had run in the 800 metres, instead of the 200 metres, as her second event she could have taken the gold or silver medal. But unfortunately Lillian will not attain her true stature as an athlete until she is coached professionally instead of by her father. Family relationships do not work in sport.

81

George was stunned. 'I've never even met the man,' he said. 'How the hell can he say I shouldn't be coaching Lillian when he doesn't even know my views and theories on athletics?

'And what's this about family relationships not working in sport? What about Della James and Janet Simpson, they're both coached by their fathers? And Robbie Brightwell helped Ann Packer before they were married.

'He must think I just stand at the side of the track shouting "C'mon our kid." '

Nor did George understand Brasher's interpretation of Lillian's state of mind before the race: '. . . she stood behind her blocks, brushed her short hair behind her ears, fiddled with her shorts, brushed her hair back again, licked her lips, touched her face. I don't think I've ever seen anyone quite so nervous at the start of any race.'

'He could never have seen you run before,' George told Lillian, 'otherwise he'd know you go through that routine before every race . . . even in training. He's had his mind fixed on a certain theme and tried to justify it.' George brooded for hours over Brasher's statements. They were unfair, but he had no way of replying.

Lillian had always been more than happy with his coaching, respecting him more than any of the national coaches. In fact, she had written to Denis Watts soon after returning from Mexico saying she wanted her father alone to deal with her training. And, surely, George felt, it was better for someone who knew the athlete's make-up to handle their training. Far better, in fact, than the kind of pressurised professional approach that had made Vera Nikolic break down in her 800 metre heats in Mexico and fly back to Belgrade on the verge of a nervous breakdown.

National coaches hadn't the time to cater for each athlete's every need. There was a battery hen style about their approach. He had been quite happy for Denis Watts to give advice on occasions; he had felt like a small businessman backed by the Bank of England. But when all was said and done, it was his business; he had built it up and it was flourishing.

Brasher's remarks had cut deep. They weren't easy to shrug aside, so George chose to use them as a spur. Every night while driving Lillian to the track for training, he would stop at a certain set of lights and mutter. 'She will not attain her true stature until she is trained professionally . . . we'll show him.'

AND SO TO ATHENS

The post-Mexico social calendar lasted well into December. As well as official functions, Lillian was invited to, and attended, all kinds of meetings and social evenings, many of them for handicapped people. She never liked to refuse, feeling herself lucky to be in a position to bring some pleasure to those less fortunate. Lillian stamped her own sparkling naturalness on the more sophisticated dinner-dances, never letting herself be overawed by the occasion or the guest list. Occasionally, too, she brought an unwitting moment of humour to supposedly serious proceedings . . . like the famous time she got up from her seat to collect an award from Lord Mountbatten and mistakenly walked straight past him. She was voted runner-up to Sheila Sherwood in the athletic writers' poll for Athlete of the Year, but won the sportswriters' award of Sportswoman of the Year.

Lillian now had a number of boy friends but usually preferred to be escorted to sports dinners by her father. On the night of the sportswriters' presentation, however, she chose to go with Bobby McGregor, the Olympic swimmer. The following day a Scottish paper reported they were engaged. A week later Lillian kicked off a charity soccer match at the request of disc jockey Ed Stewart. That evening George was pestered by enquiries as to how long Lillian and Stewart had been engaged.

'I don't know a lot about it,' George told the callers. 'But it sounds a little bit tricky as she's already engaged to Bobby McGregor, or so your colleagues tell me.'

It was a good example of the kind of limelight that was being focused on Lillian. She had long given up the hope of a break from the public eye with the end of the athletic season. She was the papers' girl for all seasons, and no longer a five months' sports item.

Lillian celebrated her twentieth birthday on December 13th with an in-depth interview with Neil Allen in *The Times*. For the first time she had an opportunity to answer back at her Mexico critics and told Allen:

'At the beginning of the year I wasn't worried at all about Press reaction. It was terribly silly of me, but I thought that if I won a gold medal you'd all write lovely things about me, but if I lost then nothing would be written about me at all. I just thought I'd be forgotten. Perhaps it was just as well I thought like that, even if it was a bit innocent.

'After I was beaten there was all this inquest stuff about "what went wrong" and why I "failed". I lose by seven-hundredths of a second and suddenly it's all a case of post-mortems. I know it doesn't really matter what the Press write, you just have to be true to yourself. But, yes, I do feel a little bitter. No, not bitter, just a shade cynical.'

Of Brasher's criticism of her father she said: 'How the dickens does he, or any of you know what's best for me. Denis Watts was marvellous as an adviser, but he lives in the north, so, naturally, I didn't see much of him. It's my father who's been coaching me for the past eight years and he's been out with me night after night.'

She ended by telling Allen she was really looking forward to the European Championships in Athens the following summer. She had decided to try and put Mexico behind her and look forward only. Her early season training, though, was interrupted by three events, one frightening, one seemingly trivial and the other of international importance.

First she began to receive a series of obscene phone calls from what sounded like a middle-aged man. They started with just heavy breathing but after a couple of weeks had progressed into a bi-weekly nightmare of foul abuse. The police were told, but George took his own action by having his telephone number changed and made ex-directory.

Soon afterwards Lillian was invited to speak at the prize-giving of her old school, the Grange. She had been to similar events dozens of times before, but this one carried special importance. She desperately wanted to go down well and spent far longer than usual preparing her speech.

'I'll bet when I was at Grange none of the teachers ever thought I'd be asked back as a guest of honour,' she told George. 'They all thought I was dim and had to have Irene to look after me. I want to show them just how wrong they were.'

And finally, she was invited to compete with a small British team in South Africa. It was a chance she had always looked forward to, right from the start of her international career. It was one of the best possible trips with only three competitions in three weeks and, more important, it would give her the chance to see the land of her birth. She accepted immediately—but then came the repercussions.

Anti-apartheid groups throughout Britain bombarded her with letters asking her not to go. Coloured athletes threatened to boycott the 1970 Commonwealth Games in Scotland if the British team did not refuse the invitation. After a lot of thought Lillian turned down the trip. 'Politics don't interest me,' she said while explaining her decision, 'but I would hate to feel responsible for ruining the Commonwealth Games.' She later came to regret the decision. For some British athletes did compete in South Africa; and no coloured athletes boycotted the Commonwealth Games.

Lillian, by now, was a fairly regular guest on T.V. shows and donated the fees to the Middlesex County Athletic Association. One tremendously successful appearance on the Dave Allen Show completed her establishment as one of Britain's most articulate and witty sports personalities. Dave Allen asked her about the Olympic sex test.

'It was a little embarrassing really,' Lillian told him and the millions of viewers. 'I didn't really know where to put my hands.'

The audience guffawed. But more was to come.

'Tell us about the tests,' Dave Allen prompted.

'There were two,' she said. 'But one of them was over in a flash.' She always maintained she had said it innocently, but the audience caught the double meaning and rocked in their seats.

Radio broadcasters, too, were quick to use her knack of saying the right thing. Jack de Manio at the B.B.C. was swiftly off the mark the day after a newspaper carried a story that some girl athletes were wearing padded bras to give themselves an unfair advantage.

His phone call brought Lillian out of bed in her curlers and dressing gown at six-thirty in the morning to tape an interview.

'Do you wear a padded bra, Lillian?' he asked.

'I take the view that I have to do without what I haven't been blessed with,' she told him.

Then, 'Is there any advantage in running with no bra?'

'Not unless you want to finish with two black eyes,' she said without a pause for thought, and de Manio put the phone down with a chuckle.

With her film star following, Lillian was swamped with offers of attractive jobs that demanded little more than her name on the letter-headings or her appearance at a few business functions. But George advised her against them. 'We've got to be realistic,' he said. 'Your name will only be worthwhile to these people all the time you're a star. Once you retire they won't want you for very long. You'll be out of a job and without a trade.'

Under his guidance, Lillian joined sportswear manufacturers Lastonet Ltd., a subsidiary of the John Heathcote Group, as a trainee designer. She had always been an expert needlewoman and made most of her own clothes. This, George felt, was the best possible craft for Lillian to learn. Once her athletic career ended she would have the self-respect of knowing that she could earn a living without using her name. So, turning down a £2,000 offer to make a television commercial and an equally lucrative one to write a string of articles for a newspaper, Lillian settled into her new job. She started by designing track-suits, making sure that they were described as 'Designed by Lillian

Board' and not 'The Lillian Board Range'—which would have been contrary to her amateur status.

The amateur laws had always annoyed George. He had long advocated that amateur status in athletics should be abandoned as in tennis. But he had always stuck rigidly to them, even to the point of turning down a handful of shillings for magazine interviews. He was well aware that some other athletes were quick to make a bit on the side, but his conscience would not let him join them.

'Good luck to them,' he told Lillian. 'I wish I could do it, perhaps then I wouldn't have to lay bricks for a living any more. But for the time being we'll play fair and hope to get back what we've turned down when you retire. The set-up's crazy at the moment but we'll have to put up with it.' So it was in amazement that he opened the *Sunday Times* and turned to the Inside Track column written that week by Dudley Doust. Under a cross-head 'Wages of Virtue' Doust had written:

That top class amateur athletes can eat their cake and have it too was lost on Dorothy Hyman, the guileless 1960 Olympic medallist who recently resurfaced as our best woman sprinter.

In 1964, Dorothy made £200 and lost her international amateur standard by helping to write a book on her career called *Sprint to Fame*. She might have signed a publisher's document falsely disclaiming such remuneration, or had the money paid over to a relative or even set up a trust fund for later collection. But she found those distasteful and refused.

On the other hand our other two great women athletes, Mary Rand and Lillian Board, by vetting their contracts with Harold Abrahams, the legal adviser to the Women's B.A.A.B., sailed skilfully close to professionalism. Mary, you'll recall, became a journalist as an amateur athlete and wrote some high-priced, non-sports rubbish for the *Sunday Mirror*. Lillian, a trainee-designer for a fabrics maker, has designed a track-suit and perks around town in a company car.

George was staggered by the article in a paper he had always gone out of his way to help. But then he saw the funny side of it. Mr Doust had let his imagination run just a little too far—for at that stage Lillian hadn't even passed her driving test.

At about this same time, George discovered a new aid for Lillian's training. It came via Roger Pedrick, a half-miler who belonged to Thames Valley Harriers and who for the past two years had helped pace Lillian through training runs whatever the weather. He was a student teacher at St Mary's College, Twickenham, and gained permission for George and Lillian to use the college training facilities any time they wished. George found these facilities included an electric cardiograph machine which recorded Lillian's heartbeat under stress. George had been hoping to use one of these for some time, but there were very few available throughout the country. Now he had found one almost on his own doorstep.

Lillian's training went from good to better. Her nightly schedules of 8 × 200 metres or 6 × 300 metres had some of the male athletes grimacing with grudging admiration at her speed and stamina. Not that George ever worked her too hard; he still held by his maxim that he was there to tone her up, not drag her down. It was just that Lillian's strength, which had been carefully built up over the years, was now showing itself fully as she matured—as George had said it would.

On May 24th, Lillian used the Middlesex Championship 800, her first race since Mexico, as an experiment. For the first time in the longer distance, she went out hard from the gun, covering the first 200 inside 28 seconds. But a combination of slow track, blustery conditions and lack of opposition held her back to 2 min 07·9 sec. Two weeks later at Reading she won her second 800 of the season in 2 min 04·8 sec after a gripping race with Rosemary Stirling. Lillian always had the utmost respect for Rosemary and freely admitted her training was far more severe than her own. Lillian's speed as well as her strength were shown over the next couple of weeks as she ran 100 metres in

11·9, 200 in 23·8 against the wind and a solo 52·9 contribution to a world 4 × 400 metre relay record.

Everything was going marvellously and she and George had decided to make the 400 metres her goal in Athens when suddenly, while running at Hendon, her back went. Training was out and she went back to the thrice-weekly visits to Ron Ettridge that she had stopped just before leaving for Mexico. Ron suggested Lillian should have a second opinion, so Harold Abrahams, chairman and legal adviser to the B.A.A.B., arranged for Lillian to visit an orthopaedic surgeon in Harley Street. He confirmed Ron Ettridge's diagnosis of strained ligaments.

George realised the trouble would be more acute in the more explosive events, so he and Lillian shifted their sights to the European 800. But even with treatment Lillian was able to train only lightly and was unable to race throughout the whole of July, which included the Women's A.A.A. championships.

She resumed competition in August and gave an amazing demonstration of her reserves of strength by defying the enforced lay-off to clock a 52·5 400 metre winning relay leg in a match between Great Britain and the U.S.A. at the White City. She followed this the next day with an individual 53·7 to finish second to America's quarter-mile star Kathy Hammond (53·1). Considering the fact that Lillian's usual style of going out fast from the blocks had been made impossible by her injury, they were magnificent performances. Three days later came the chance Lillian had waited ten months for—Great Britain versus France at Middlesborough and a revenge meeting with Colette Besson over 400.

Colette was in superb form and Lillian, still feeling under par, gave herself little chance. 'I'm going to start as fast as I dare with my back,' she told George, 'and then hope to beat her on strength in the home straight.' She did just as she had promised and rounded the first bend in the lead and against a strong wind. Lillian sensed it would not be a fast time in view of the conditions, but realised that was all to her benefit. She had been forced to train purely for stamina in recent weeks and now, she hoped, it would pay off. She gave it everything she had against the wind, eased off round the last bend and then kicked hard. She won in 53·7 with Besson second 54·1 and Janet Simpson third 54·9. Roy Moor, athletics writer from the *Daily Mail*, was the first to congratulate Lillian as she hugged George excitedly. 'That was a bold and courageous run,' he said. 'I must admit most of us hadn't given you a lot of chance.'

Her last race in England before leaving for Athens was an 800 metres at Crystal Palace on August 27th. She won in 2 min 05·1 sec with a fiery second lap of 60·3. George was growing more and more confident about her chances in the European Championships, but he said little to Lillian. She was ranked eighth in the world over 800 on her season's showing, so she was going into the championships with none of the pressures that had surrounded her in Mexico— and he wanted to keep it that way.

Lillian, too, was busy with other matters outside athletics and had had little time to dwell on her prospects. She had been busy taking driving lessons throughout the early summer and had been desperate to pass first time as brother George and Irene had done before her. She had succeeded —although she kidded her family for an hour that she had failed. But no sooner was that over than she found herself landed with the job of compering a West End fashion show which was displaying her first attempts at designing sports and casual wear.

As accustomed as she was to public speaking, Lillian was anxious for the show to be a success. She had chosen to be a designer, so her personality demanded she did well at it. In fact, it went off better than she could have hoped. Fashion expert Norman Hartnell, commenting on her designs, wrote: 'She is way ahead of her rivals—both as a runner and a designer. Until now, most athletics sportswear has been streamlined and functional. Thanks to Lillian, however, athletics gear has suddenly become glamorous.' By the time the show was over, Lillian had just two days left in which to prepare to leave for Athens. 'After what I've been through, running will seem easy,' she told George. 'At least I know I can do that fairly well.'

Lillian was captivated immediately by the beauty of Greece. She loved its gay, stirring music and revelled in its deep, historic undertones. This was where athletics all started, she thought. The conception of the Olympics was born here. She found her surroundings both elating and relaxing, a strange combination which filled her with the conviction that the championships held in store great things for her. Her feelings were strengthened in her 800 metre heat. She nodded off to sleep shortly before the start and woke to run a relaxed race and win in a season's best—2 min. 04·2 sec. But still she was not hailed as a potential gold medallist. That tag was being shared between Rumania's Olympic bronze medallist Ileana Silać and Vera Nikolic, the Yugoslavian world record holder.

The following day, on the eve of the final, she telephoned George as arranged at the hotel in which he and Frances were staying with another party from *Athletics Weekly*. Irene had remained at home. Lillian was still thrilled about her run the day before.

George told her, 'Play it safe in the final tomorrow. Keep on the shoulder of the leader until the last bend and then let it rip. Don't worry about the outcome, just do your best and that'll be good enough for me.'

'Oh, but I want to win a medal,' Lillian said with a trace of disappointment. 'Don't you think I've got a chance then?'

'Listen,' George said firmly. 'I was just trying to make it easy for you. Of course you have a chance of a medal. In fact, I've got news for you—you're going to win.'

Lillian sighed with relief. 'I'm so glad you've said that. You had me worried for a minute.'

As George put the phone down he knew the gold was as good as won. But he still refused to make predictions in the Press. *Daily Mirror* correspondent Frank Taylor, a long-standing friend of George's and a fellow Lancastrian, tapped him the same evening.

'Well, George old pal,' he said in his slow, relaxed voice, 'what's she going to do?'

'As you know Frank, she's been worried by this injury,' George replied cagily. 'She's got no real form and no one seems to be giving her a chance.'

'Aye, I know. But what's she going to do?'

'Well, Frank,' George said with a trace of a smug smile, 'let's just say she'll be thereabouts.'

An hour before the race Frances sat in the grandstand of the packed arena feeling the tension building up inside her. She so desperately wanted Lillian to do well to make up for her disappointment in the Olympics. She could feel her head swimming with the heat and the claustrophobic closeness of the massed thousands around her. She tried to ignore it and peered towards the tunnel through which the athletes entered the stadium. Suddenly everything went hazy . . .

George, feeling Frances fall against him, was momentarily scared. Then he realised she had fainted. He tried in vain to revive her and decided he would have to take her to the first aid room . . . but how? It was underneath the stadium and every exit way was packed with spectators. Phil Vivien, secretary of Thames Valley Harriers and a member of the *Athletics Weekly* party, saw George's predicament and immediately came to help. Together they carried Frances slowly through the crowds. Mrs Violet Simpson, a former Olympic athlete and mother of Lillian's international colleague Janet, followed them down and sat with Frances as the first aid staff tried to bring her round. George was caught in a dilemma. There was less than half an hour now before Lillian's race. He couldn't leave Frances, but he couldn't miss the race. Lillian would look for him and Frances in the crowd as soon as she came out and would worry if she couldn't see them.

Lillian, oblivious of the drama, was worried by only one thing, that Vera Nikolic would go out fast from the start. If she did she would be left with the dreadful choice between letting her go and hoping she tired or chasing after her and risking blowing up herself.

She walked into the stadium and immediately looked for her parents. Yes, there they were, and she waved cheerfully.

George, holding tightly on to Frances who had recovered with just minutes to spare, breathed a sigh of relief.

As Lillian stood waiting for the gun she offered a silent prayer. 'Please God,' she thought, 'please don't let Vera go out fast.'

The gun went—and Nikolic settled down quietly. Lillian breathed her thanks and moved on to her shoulder. She stumbled slightly at the 400 mark and dropped back to third behind the co-favourites Nikolic and Silać. The order was the same 200 metres further on, but suddenly Lillian was feeling tired.

In her own words she described the rest of the race like this:

I realised the pace was quickening and forced myself to quicken too. Any bit of advice anyone had ever given me seemed to flash through my mind in the next few seconds, but mostly I could hear my father saying 'Keep with the leaders. Keep with the leaders and if you are with them at the 100 mark you'll win.'

Ileana and Vera were still moving away. 'You must keep with them . . . you must.' I pulled back a little and was with them at the 100 mark. Something screamed at me, 'Now you must go . . . go on, now!' I swung wide into lane three and went. Suddenly I was past them, I was clear and the tape was getting nearer. 'Please don't let them catch me,' I cried to myself. 'Please don't let them catch me.'

To the watching thousands it was a massacre. Lillian powered through the tape a clear ten yards ahead of the world's best half milers for a time of 2 min 1·4 sec. Anneliese Damm-Neilsen of Denmark was second (2:02·6) and Nikolic third (2:02·6). The first 400 had been covered in 59·2 and the 600 reached in 90 seconds. If it had not been for a strong head wind in the final straight the world record must surely have been in danger.

It was a moment of supreme glory which washed away the last bitter tastes of Mexico. Lillian was running better than ever, despite her long lay off and her confidence had never been greater. It was in that frame of mind that she lined up for the 4 × 400 metre relay run the following day and the performance for which she will probably be best remembered.

In the relay final Britain were pitted against France and on paper stood no chance. Two of the French girls, Nicole Duclos and Lillian's old rival Colette Besson, were by then co-holders of the world 400 metre record with 51·7. But superb running by the other British girls, Rosemary Stirling, Pat Lowe and Janet Simpson, allowed Janet to hand over the baton to Lillian on the anchor leg less than two yards down on Besson. By 300 metres, though, the French girl had stretched the lead to ten yards, and the race seemed over. Lillian had gone through the first 200 in 24·2—her fastest ever—in a 400 race and been forced to ease off. But as they reached the home straight she began to close the gap and in a lung-bursting final effort caught Besson on the line by the same margin she had been beaten in the Mexico final the previous year.

It was a double gold medal performance which earned Lillian the supreme accolade of 'Best Woman Athlete in the Games'.

Lillian savoured her elation again later that night when, as usual, she returned to the stadium to look at the deserted track and remember moment by moment what had passed only a few hours before.

Lillian off to a good start in her heat of the 400 m. at the Mexico Olympics, 1968.

Colette Besson just pips Lillian at the post in the final.

The return from Mexico, (*above*) with John and Sheila Sherwood and David Hemery; (*below left*) a welcome hug from Irene; (*below right*) the silver medal she said she'd spray gold.

Lillian, an accomplished designer and dressmaker, on a Tailor and Cutter course.

Twin sisters, Irene and Lillian, 1970.

Sweet revenge for Mexico as Lillian beats Colette Besson at Middlesbrough, five weeks before the European Games at Athens.

Getting acclimatised in the Athletic 'village' before the European Championships in Athens, 1969, (*From the left*) Rita Ridley, Maureen Barton and Lillian.

The 4 × 400 m.
at Athens.
Lillian (*above*)
takes over from
Janet Simpson
for the last leg
and (*below*)
snatches victory
from Colette
Besson in a
world record
time of
3 min. 30.8 sec.

One foot on the ground between them, as Vera Nikolic, world record holder, leads the field in the 800 m. at Athens.

...ctory in Athens. (*Above*) Lillian wins the
...o m. in 2 min. 1.4 sec. How easily can be
...n (*right*) by the relaxed wave seconds after
...asting the tape. (*Below*) The world record
...eakers in the 4 × 400 m. (*From the left*)
...llian Board, Rosemary Stirling, Pat Lowe
...d Janet Simpson.

Lillian with the 800 m. trophy (*left*) and her two gold medals from Athens

Lillian, the torchbearer, at the Nos Galan race, Mountain Ash, Glamorgan.

PART TWO

OUR FIRST MEETING

I met Lillian the following December at the Sportswriters' annual dinner in the Bloomsbury Centre Hotel, London. And, like the rest of our relationship that first meeting carried an element of fate.

Up until two days before the dinner I was due to go with a casual girl friend but a sudden difference of opinion between us left me holding a spare ticket. Brian Woolnough, a friend of mine on the sports desk at the *Evening Post*, Hemel Hempstead, where I was then working, bought the ticket and we decided to make the most of the evening as a stag do.

We drove slowly to London that night via a few pubs as preparation for the free reception at the Martini Terrace which was to start the function. After a couple of pints Brian announced he would dance with Virginia Wade if she was there and, like hundreds of others must have done before me, I said I would ask Lillian Board. The reception and the call of the hotel bar ended Brian's half of the bargain, though, and it was only when I saw Lillian sitting almost by herself on the top table mid-way through the evening that I remembered what I had jokingly said. There seemed little to lose by now, so I made as steady a track as possible towards her. She seemed genuinely pleased to be asked to dance and I was immediately impressed by her natural friendliness and complete lack of airs and graces.

'I'm sorry,' she said as we started to dance, 'but I don't recognise you. Are you a sportsman?'

'No, I'm a sports reporter,' I told her. 'Why, what do you do?'

'I'm Lillian Board, an athlete.'

Her candour and genuine modesty made me instantly regret my feeble attempt to be funny. She was certainly different from many of the personalities I had met in the past.

'Where do you work?' she asked. And I tried to tell her. But *The Hemel Hempstead Evening Post* is difficult to say with the clearest of heads. I started twice and then gave it up as a bad job.

'*The Evening Post*,' I conceded.

'Oh, really?'

'Why, do you know it?'

'Yes, of course. I've run a few times in Birmingham. I know the *Birmingham Evening Post* well.' Fair enough, I thought and forgot about it. And in fact, it wasn't until we had been going out together for about a fortnight that Lillian finally discovered where I worked.

We danced twice more that evening and each time I could feel a growing sense of affinity. Lillian was to tell me later that by the end of the night she felt she had known me months. Finally, I decided it was pointless leaving it as a passing encounter. 'You've probably been asked this dozens of times on the dance floor by strangers, but would you come out with me some time?' I asked. 'Don't hesitate to say no if you don't want to, I'll understand.'

She stopped dancing and looked me straight in the face for about two seconds. 'All right,' she said at last, and gave me her phone number. Like all good journalists, I had no pen on me. 'You'll never remember it,' she said as I took her back to her seat.

But I did. And six weeks later, after three phone calls, we finally arranged a date for January 15th, shortly after she had been awarded the M.B.E. in the New Year Honours.

I booked a table at an Italian restaurant-cum-nightclub a few miles from Lillian's home in Ealing, London, and arrived at her house at eight p.m. with the sort of nerves I hadn't experienced since my first date. I decided I had better cut down on my smoking and pretend to be almost teetotal so as to give a reasonable impression to Lillian and her family. For, surely, they would all be fitness fanatics, buying only the right foods and doing physical jerks every morning?

Irene opened the door when I knocked and ushered me into the front room. 'Lillian's not quite ready yet. Would you like a gin and tonic while you're waiting? And do you smoke? Here, take one of these.' I had a quick check of the number on the gate, assured myself I was in the right house and settled down to wait.

Lillian came into the room twenty minutes later. 'Sorry,' she said breathlessly. 'But that's the trouble with being an athlete—training every night.' I led her to my hastily-cleaned car and drove quickly to the restaurant in order to be on time for the table reservation. She made expert small talk throughout the journey with an ease which belied her twenty-one years. It was Lillian at her most sophisticated, a side of her I was to see only rarely again—and then at official functions.

Despite Irene's welcome, I was still sure Lillian would not drink alcohol, a feeling which seemed to be borne out when she declined a drink as starters when we arrived at the restaurant. I decided in that case it would only be fair for me to forgo my celebration glass of wine during the meal. But as the wine-waiter turned to leave with barely-disguised disgust Lillian said quietly and with obvious disappointment, 'Don't you like wine?' Thereafter the evening went well. Lillian revealed a liking for gin and tonic which made me forget all my own resolutions and in the end I was forced to borrow £1 from her to leave a tip.

The myth I had built in my own mind had been well and truly exploded. Lillian was a normal, happy girl from a normal, happy family. True, she didn't smoke but that was as much out of dislike of cigarettes as any athletic principle. She enjoyed life to the full, the same as any attractive 21-year-old girl, but coupled this with tremendous natural athletic ability plus complete dedication during her nightly training sessions.

During the next month I took her out twice more and each time we grew closer. Eventually I was seeing her every weekend. I discovered that far from expecting to be taken to expensive places, Lillian preferred simple things: visiting friends, going to the cinema, chatting in country pubs. 'I have to go to so many official receptions and dinners,' she told me, 'that it's nice to be able to go out and do ordinary things.'

She was also, essentially a home-loving person. 'People seem surprised when I tell them I'm still living at home,' she told me during our second date. 'But I love my parents and the family life. I wouldn't want to swap that for a flat just for the sake of a bit more independence. When I get off the train every night I think "Oh, good, people will be in and I can talk to them about what's happened today" rather than go back to an empty room. And it's the same whenever I go away on trips. It doesn't matter how plush the hotel is or how fabulous the climate, I'm still happy to get back to my own house and my own bedroom.'

This did not really surprise me, for I had heard a Desert Island Discs programme on the radio when Lillian was the guest. The overriding theme throughout her chosen records —which included Guantanamera—was her closeness with her family, especially her father. And in fact, when at the end of the programme she had been asked to select one book to take with her as a castaway, she had chosen a family photograph album.

Wherever we went Lillian was an instant success. She had the ability to mix in any company thanks to her genuine fondness of people—apart from flatterers and hangers-on, whom she despised. A friend of mine summed it up, 'She is probably the nicest person I have met,' he said. And the same was true for me. Apart from all her other qualities, she epitomised the word my English teachers had told me never to use—she was just plain nice.

Our weekly meetings were too infrequent for both of us. But there was little we could do about it, Lillian's training and my night-time reporting assignments ruled out week-days. It did mean, however, that our Saturday and Sunday nights grew progressively later with Lillian often arriving home at three a.m. Each time it happened I felt anxious that it might harm her athletics and each time I told myself that next week we must get back earlier. But we never did and gradually a few storm clouds gathered. Lillian never mentioned a word of it to me, but one night Irene said quietly, 'You really must try to cut down on these late nights. I know it must be Lillian's fault as much as yours, but there have been a few rows about it just lately. I'm sure you can understand the position.'

And, of course, I could. After nine years of steering his daughter's athletic career, George was hardly likely to want to see it all thrown away through a few late nights now she was at the very top. Also, neither George nor Frances knew me very well at that time and I could quite understand if they felt I was just a glory hunter trying to find some reflected fame in dating a famous girl. For my part I would have been happier if Lillian's surname had been Smith. The problems of falling in love with a national figure far outweighed the pleasures.

There was the lack of privacy; the constant leg-pulling, funny to start with and gradually growing more irritating; and sometimes the embarrassment. For how do you excuse yourself from company when you're on your way to a date? You can't say, 'Got to go, I'm meeting my girl friend' because that's an understatement. You can only say, 'I'm going to meet Lillian' to people who already know you are going out with her. You can never say, 'I'm going to meet Lillian Board' because that's conceited. So usually you settle for plain 'Got to go' and get labelled as unsociable.

Nor did Lillian's athletic prowess influence my feelings towards her. I was simply happy if she was happy and if that included running, then that was fine. It was an attitude she seemed to find unusual and in a way that made me glad. 'So many people I've known are only interested in me because I win races,' she said. 'Sometimes I'm scared that no one will like me when I retire from athletics.' I told her time and again that this was rubbish; that she might be *respected* because of her success, but she was *liked* because of her personality. But she was never entirely convinced.

*   *   *

At this time I was living in Aldbury, a small village about ten miles from Hemel Hempstead. It was a close-knit community and I had been there at least six months before I felt anywhere near accepted by the majority of the residents. Lillian captured them in one evening. Jack Dunne, an ex-mining engineer who owned the local pub, 'The Grey-hound', told me after twice meeting Lillian, 'She's so full of life it's incredible. Looking at her you'd never think she could be unhappy. She's one big smile all the time; she just fills the place with sunshine.'

It was an attitude shared by all my friends in the village, especially David Price, known throughout the area as 'Podge'. A former public schoolboy, he worked as a free-lance car salesman and had befriended me the previous summer when I had broken my leg and was unable to drive from my digs in Luton to work. He put me up in his cottage and carried me around rather like a lame dog. He had a keen wit and instantly appreciated Lillian's ability to see the funny side in most situations.

'Why do you call yourself "Podge"?' she asked almost as soon as she'd met him.

'Because I was fat as a baby,' he said. 'But then I caught a serious illness.'

Lillian was deeply concerned. 'Scarlet fever? Diphtheria?'

'No, it was called growing up.'

They got on famously after that and any weekend that we didn't have commitments in London we would travel to Aldbury for one of the endless streams of parties. 'She really is a super girl,' Podge told me in one of his rare moments of seriousness. 'She's the kind of girl everybody should marry.'

I had known Lillian for about two months when I was offered a job on the *Daily Mail* sports desk. She was the first person I rang with the news and she made me feel as if I had broken a world record and won a gold medal into the bargain. She was so pleased for me and made it sound such a fantastic accomplishment that I grew a bit embarrassed. 'C'mon,' I told her, 'compared to your achievements it doesn't even rate a word in the small print.' But she wouldn't listen. 'Rubbish,' she said. 'This is your career. It's much more important than anybody's sporting achievements.'

I doubted she meant all she was saying, but in her usual way she was doing a first class P.R.O. job for my ego and I couldn't pretend I didn't like it. Because however much I told myself that famous names and high positions in life didn't cut much ice with me, I still had a few sneaking feelings of inferiority about going out with Lillian. I knew that to a lot of people I would just be 'Lillian Board's boy friend' and any little thing I could do to even the balance would be healthy for both of us. As a Fleet Street journalist I at least had one foot on the ladder to social equality with her. The change brought its fresh batch of problems, though. Apart from the strange feeling of dealing with stories directly concerned with Lillian and a dread that some people might think I was going out with her just to further my career, there was also a difference in working hours. I was now on nights, including Sundays, and that meant that the only possible time I could see her was on Saturdays or my one free night in the week if her training schedule allowed. There was one main advantage, however, and that was that I had ample time to pursue a secret ambition—and get fit again. It was bad enough going out with a girl who could beat me in a race for a bus. To think she could give me a lap start and probably still thrash me over half a mile was unbearable.

I stopped smoking and went daily to a small running track just outside London. And it was only then that I began to appreciate fully just how much effort Lillian had put into getting to the top. I had watched a couple of her training sessions and knew the broad outline of most of her schedules. In glorious ignorance I was sure I would be able to manage some of them after a fortnight's limbering up.

But even if the mind was willing, and that was sometimes sorely in doubt, the flesh was incapable. After a month's hard slog that completely ruined my digestive system all I had to show was two blistered feet, a couple of excruciatingly bruised shin-bones and a few appalling lap times which my sister had clocked in between bouts of helpless laughter on a beautifully sunny day that I had earmarked as my moment of truth.

Lillian's training, meantime, was going fairly well. She told me that even if the occasional late nights were taking a toll, it was more than made up for by her tremendously happy frame of mind.

Her first race of the season was at Watford on May 2nd and although it was only a club meeting the magic of her name drew hundreds of spectators. Lillian had been undecided whether she wanted me to go along or not. 'I'm always nervous for the first race of the season,' she said. 'If I know you're there as well it will make it even worse.' I told her I would probably have to work that afternoon anyway, but arrived just after the meeting had started and picked a seat well at the back of the stand.

It was a strange feeling sitting there watching Lillian sign autographs, pose for photographs and chat with the officials. Suddenly she was no longer my girl friend, she was the public's sweetheart and I felt almost like a usurper. This was Lillian the athlete, the national personality, and it was difficult to realise she was the same girl who always insisted on doing a bit of housework whenever she visited my digs. If there was any barrier between us, this was it. Part of her would always belong to the public and would I, who had never experienced that kind of adulation or shouldered that sort of responsibility, ever fully understand that side of her?

I had experienced the same feeling to a lesser degree when strangers came up to us in restaurants or in the street to pay their respects and wish Lillian the best of luck for the new season. One moment I was talking to Lillian, my girl friend, the next I was talking to Lillian Board, public celebrity. But through all my mixed emotions as I sat in Watford on that Saturday afternoon, the ones that stood out strongest were pride and admiration. Before then I had seen Lillian run only on television. To watch her in person was a fantastic experience, for there was no question of it, she was superb. The magnetism of her running proved expensive, however. I had been given a strong tip for the 3.30 at Windsor but completely forgot about it as Lillian prepared to line up for the 400 metres. She won easily and so did the horse—at 4 to 1.

I left my seat at the end of the race and walked down to the grassy edge of the running track where she was talking to George and Frances. She was surprised and pleased to see me, but was disappointed over her performance. It had seemed excellent to me for the first time out against relatively poor opposition, but Lillian was a perfectionist. She embodied George's oft-declared principle, 'Most people aim for the moon and fall short. We aim a foot above the moon, so if we fall short we're still higher than anyone else.'

Listening to George talk on athletics was fascinating and I was glad I knew a little about the subject, especially in the early days of going out with Lillian, when he would sit me down and discuss various training theories while I was waiting for her to get ready. I found him instantly likeable, with a keen sense of humour and a colourful turn of phrase which combined his naval war service with Lancastrian humour. Even so, in those days I was never sure just how he felt about me, knowing his feelings about the Press. I had the impression he liked me but I was a threat to Lillian's career and as such not really to be encouraged. As time went by, though, he began to understand me better, thanks partly to Lillian's prompting, and we developed a fine relationship. Frances, I always felt, was my ally, and apart from one occasion, when she read the riot act about late nights, always seemed happy that Lillian and I were getting on so well.

As the athletics season warmed up, one of the main topics of conversation in Lillian's house was, 'Just how good is Marilyn Neufville going to be this year?' Still only a schoolgirl, Jamaican-born Marilyn had landed some impressive

400 metre victories at indoor meetings during the winter. Lillian's avowed aim for the season was the 800 metre Commonwealth Games Games title and a lowering of the world record to below two minutes. But I knew that George had a double target of 400 and 800 metres at the back of his mind for the 1972 Munich Olympics. I knew also that Lillian would not opt out of a clash with Marilyn sometime in the season even if her training was not geared for peak 400 metre performances. George realised Neufville's great potential, but was not unduly worried.

'Lillian's never reached her peak over 400,' he told me. 'In fact, she's never had a chance to show her full potential over any distance. She's always had such a great range of ability that we've never been able to concentrate solely on one event. She could have been world class over 200, but we moved on to the 400. She set the British record, ran the third fastest time in the world, won an Olympic silver over that distance and then we went up to the 800.

'This season she's going to try a few 1500 metres, partly because it's good over-distance for the 800 and partly because no one has ever represented Britain at all distances before. It would be a marvellous achievement—and the 1500's the only one Lillian's got left.

'This means that we'll have very little time to concentrate on the 400 and a probable show-down with Neufville. We'll just have to hope that Lillian's 800 metre training carries her through.'

Lillian's first outing in her challenge for a 1500 metre international vest was in a British Milers' Club mile at the West London Stadium. She finished third, despite the handicap of an upset stomach which was nothing to do with her later illness, but clocked a useful 4 min 55·7 sec. She was disappointed over her performance, but it was good enough to earn her selection for an international mile in Rome the following weekend. Among the opposition was Paola Pigni of Italy, the former world record holder.

George saw her off to the airport with the prediction, 'You'll knock a good ten seconds off last week's performance.' In fact, she trimmed 11·1 seconds and finished second to Pigni. Once again George had proved his wisdom, for he made a fierce point of never telling Lillian anything he did not know was true.

'It's all a question of trust,' he confided once. 'Whatever I tell Lillian she knows I believe it. It's no good building her up on lies, she'd soon realise what I was up to. I'd rather tell her she's going to lose than tell her she'll win if I don't think she will. If she does win then she's doubly happy. If she loses then she'll believe me next time when I tell her she's going to win.'

I met Lillian at the airport when she flew back on the Sunday. I'd rarely seen her so elated. She was full of the race. 'It was so different from last week,' she said. 'These miles make me so nervous I often wonder if they're worth the trouble. It seems such a long way when you're about to start the race. But now I've done one well it's made it all worth while.' For the rest of the afternoon I'd lost her completely to athletics. She talked about the trip, about her companions and the sightseeing tour of Rome. I started to feel just a little left out, but stifled the thought, telling myself that Lillian's happiness was the most important thing.

It was in the next two weeks that Lillian started to get the first of her stomach upsets. She visited her local doctor who diagnosed a virus and gave her a prescription for pills. The trouble seemed to clear slightly and Lillian got down to the job of preparing for her much-publicised clash with Marilyn Neufville in the Southern Counties Championships at Crystal Palace on May 30th. She had difficulty keeping to her training schedule, but refused to think about pulling out mainly through hatred of being called a coward.

Marilyn won in what would have been a new British record of 52 seconds but for her flying start. Lillian finished second in 53·6, partly because she had held back, waiting for a false start to be declared. She would make no excuses, though. 'She beat me, that was all. But it might be a different story later in the season,' was all she would say.

As the days went by, Lillian's discomfort grew. But on June 13th she still managed to go to the Meadowbank

Stadium, Edinburgh, for the Commonwealth Games preview and help set a 4 × 800 metres world record with a last leg of 2 min 6·8 sec.

Lillian's next major event was the Women's A.A.A. 800 metres at Crystal Palace the following week. But when the evening of the heats arrived on the Friday, she was doubled up in pain on her bed. George and Frances tried to persuade her not to take part but she doggedly refused to pull out. 'This is my last chance to qualify for the Commonwealth Games,' she said. 'I must at least run in tonight's heats.' And so she did, winning her heat in what, under the circumstances, was the amazing time of 2 min 6·8 sec. It had been a tremendous strain on her but she continued to carry off the act in the post-race interviews. 'How's your bug?' one of the reporters asked. 'Fine, thanks,' said Lillian. 'How's yours?' It was George who finally had to put the record straight. 'She won't tell you this herself,' he told the Press men. 'But up until half an hour before the race she was in agony. I told her not to run but she was scared to pull out in case people thought she was making excuses.'

Lillian's condition, which we put down to a form of gastro-enteritis, was no better by the morning. But again she was determined to take part in the afternoon's final. She defied all the odds to run a superb race but her legs lacked their usual spring in the final 150 yards and she finished third to Sheila Carey. She again put on a brave face for the Press but as I drove her home that night she cried in front of me for the first time. 'It's not so much losing,' she said. 'It's the way it happened. I wouldn't mind if they were better than me. But I'm sure I could beat them if only I wasn't ill.' As we reached her house she added, 'This bug's getting worse, you know. I wonder if it will stop me running in the Commonwealth Games.'

But then her face brightened a little as she said the words which will always haunt me. 'I suppose I could be out for the whole season. But that wouldn't be so bad, would it? At least you and I would have more time together.'

10

THE DIAGNOSIS

The following week we arranged for Lillian to have X-rays at Acton Hospital. These proved inconclusive and a few days later I drove her to Central Middlesex Hospital for a second series. I sat with Lillian in the reception hall as we waited for the results. The pains that had plagued her the previous week had now eased slightly, but she was still feeling a little shaky, both from the after-effects and the vast amount of barium meal she had had to drink for X-ray purposes. Finally, we were called in to see the woman radiologist. I could see from the stern expression on her face that things were worse than I had suspected.

'You realise this is quite serious, do you?' she asked Lillian. 'You have an inflammation of some sort in the bowel. But without an internal examination I can't say exactly what is wrong. In the meantime you must rest.'

From what I knew of hospitals I realised that for this sort of information to be volunteered, Lillian's condition must be serious. But Lillian had missed the implications. She seemed quite happy on the way home and was even wondering if she could carry on training.

'It's the Commonwealth Games in a fortnight's time,' she said. 'I can't start to miss training now.'

'You're going home to rest,' I said, trying to sound firm without giving her cause for alarm. 'We want to get this thing cleared up quickly. It's no good going out and straining yourself at this stage.'

She seemed reluctant, but Frances backed up what I had

said when we got home and she waited impatiently for the next examination a couple of days later. This time we returned to Acton Hospital for Lillian to see Dr Ewart Jepson. She was gone for about half an hour and came back looking a little shaken.

'They want me to come into hospital,' she said.

'When?'

'Today, now, as soon as possible. I've got something called Crohn's Disease, whatever that is. And it seems I've definitely got to miss the Commonwealth Games.'

And then Lillian remembered something else which she made sound equally important. 'It's your night off tonight, isn't it? And you were going to take me to see *Dr Zhivago*. Oh, well that settles it, I'm not going into hospital today. *Dr Zhivago* tonight, Dr Jepson tomorrow.'

Frances, Irene and myself took Lillian to hospital the following day. She had been given a private room and the hospital secretary assured us we would be able to visit any time we wished. I stayed on after the others had left for work. 'This is the second time I've stayed in hospital,' Lillian told me. 'A couple of years ago I had to have an impacted wisdom tooth out and they kept me in a couple of days. But they put me in the gynaecological ward—and that caused a few raised eyebrows I can tell you.'

She was philosophical about missing the Games. 'It's not as if they're the Olympics,' she said. 'But it will be funny lying here while all the others are up in Edinburgh. And it is my last chance of winning a Commonwealth medal. But at least now everybody knows I wasn't just making excuses for being beaten, there is something wrong with me.'

Lillian stayed in Acton for ten days, watching the Games from her bed on a television hired by the hospital. The doctors seemed quite happy about her condition. 'We're ninety-nine per cent certain it's Crohn's,' one of them told George. 'It's an unusual complaint in young people. We're hoping to reduce the inflammation with medicine and without using surgery.'

Near the end of her stay in hospital Lillian was warned the disease might mean the finish of her international career. 'Apparently this can keep on flaring up unless I keep to a rigid diet and don't exert myself too much,' she explained. 'But it wouldn't be too terrible, would it? I have to retire sometime and there's other things in life besides athletics.'

Lillian was released from hospital with several bottles of pills and orders to rest and eat only easily digestible foods. The pain in her stomach had become a constant ache which sometimes gave way to severe cramps but she would suffer it all without complaint. Sometimes she would suddenly disappear as we sat watching television and I would find her half an hour later lying quietly on her bed.

'Why didn't you tell me you weren't feeling well?' I would ask.

'I hate to keep on complaining. There's nothing worse than someone who keeps on moaning. Leave me alone and I'll be all right in a few minutes.'

After being confined in hospital for nearly two weeks, Lillian was anxious to get out a bit. But even short walks or attempted shopping expeditions tired her and brought on bouts of stomach cramp. Her condition deteriorated more sharply in the third week and Frances arranged for Lillian to see Sir Francis Avery-Jones, one of the country's foremost specialist authorities on enteritis, who had confirmed the original diagnosis of Crohn's. He was a consultant at Acton, but his main office was at Central Middlesex Hospital and it was there we went for the check-up.

'I'm afraid you will have to come back into hospital,' he told Lillian. 'The trouble has flared up again and I think now it's a bit worse than it was.'

The following day Lillian was admitted to St Mark's Hospital, City Road, Islington. Sir Francis said that an operation might now be necessary. The infection was causing a blockage and if this did not ease it would have to be cut out. In the meantime Lillian would almost certainly have to have a temporary colotomy.

On Thursday, September 3rd, five days after Lillian moved into St Mark's, Sir Francis telephoned me at the *Evening News* where I was working a day shift. 'I'm very sorry to have to tell you this,' he said. 'But we will have to operate on Lillian this afternoon to perform a temporary colotomy.'

I knew Lillian, like myself, had a dread of surgery, so I immediately rang my mother and asked her to go to the hospital. Lillian and she were very close and as my mother had undergone an operation a few years previous I felt she would be able to ease Lillian's fear of the unknown. I reached the hospital a couple of hours later, just after my mother had left. Lillian was starting to feel the effects of the pre-operation drugs.

'I was terrified at first,' she told me. 'But I realise it's got to be done. They've told me it's one of the smallest operations possible, far less complicated than even an appendicitis.' I stayed with her until it was time for her to be taken to the theatre. 'At least it will probably ease some of the pain,' Lillian told me almost by way of reassurance as she was wheeled out of the ward. 'And anyway, it's only temporary.'

I telephoned the hospital later that afternoon and they told me all had gone well and I could visit Lillian the same evening. She looked very pale and tired as I squeezed between the partitioning curtains. I had expected this, but I was still shocked by her utter helplessness. 'It hurts so much more than I thought it would,' she told me in a whisper. 'I can't talk, it's too painful.' I sat with her until she drifted into sleep and suddenly I had a mental picture of how she had been only a month ago. How must she feel? I asked myself. One moment her life was filled with activity and ambition. Now she lay in a hospital bed, weak and in pain; her athletics career almost certainly over before it had really begun; the prospect of at least one more operation; and no certain knowledge that she was getting any better.

The idea of the colotomy repelled Lillian at first, but she gradually learnt to live with it. I asked to see what it looked like after a couple of days, thinking that if Lillian realised I found it perfectly acceptable she would not mind it so much herself. She removed the dressing to reveal the incision where the intestine had been brought to the outside of her stomach. 'There's nothing wrong with that,' I told her. 'It's exactly what I'm like inside anyway. We'll call it Fred from now on.' The idea appealed to her and each day she would give me a bulletin on Fred's progress. Soon after the colotomy operation the doctors stopped calling Lillian's condition Crohn's Disease and restyled it 'a stricture'.

Sir Francis Avery-Jones had left for a visit to Australia the day after Lillian's operation so most of my information came from Lillian's surgeon, Mr Peter Hawley. He explained there was a blockage in the rectum which they were trying to reduce through treatment. Once it had shrunk they would remove it by surgery and join the healthy parts together. The danger was that the stricture might be too near the end of the rectum and this would mean Lillian having a permanent colotomy.

The weeks went by and Lillian's gradual loss of weight over the previous month started to accelerate. It had made her even more attractive at first, but now it was alarming— and apart from a couple of exploratory biopsies there seemed little action by the hospital. Then, mid-way through the fifth week I arrived for my usual couple of hours' visiting in the afternoon to find Lillian obviously upset. 'They tell me I'll probably have to have a permanent colotomy,' she said, and her eyes searched my face for a reaction.

I had been half expecting this news for some time and I knew it was essential Lillian must be reassured immediately. One slip now and she would be feeling inferior for the rest of her life.

'That's not so terrible, though, is it?' I said. 'Lots of people have them and you never know the difference. There are some film stars and other famous people who have colotomies.' I gave her a few names, some I knew to be true, others I made up.

'It's only a little thing, anyway, just like a small scar on the side of your stomach.'

She was looking at me intently. 'Have you seen anyone on the way in here? Have they told you what to say?'

'Of course not. None of the doctors are around. I didn't know anything about this until you told me.'

'But what about you? How do you feel about it?'

'Me? What do you mean? If you mean as far as my feelings towards you are concerned, then it doesn't make the slightest difference. In fact, you must think I'm a pretty shallow sort of person, if you were scared it would make a difference. You're just the same, colotomy or not.'

The relief spread across her face and as I held her to me I could feel the tears in her eyes. 'It doesn't matter to me if I have a colotomy,' she said in a rush. 'Oh, God, don't you get your priorities straightened out when this sort of thing happens? Running round a track for a bit of tin and your picture in the paper. What does it matter? Health is the important thing. Health and sharing your life with someone.'

'I'll see Mr Hawley this Saturday,' I said, 'and find out just what's happening and when. If it's got to be done it might as well be soon and then you can get out of this place and maybe we'll even manage a holiday before the summer ends.'

I saw a couple of the nurses on the way out. 'Do you know exactly what's happening.' I asked them. They had rather a strange, embarrassed look on their faces.

'Have you seen the doctor?' one of them asked.

'No, I'm seeing him this Saturday.'

'Oh well, he knows more about it than we do. He'll be able to tell you everything.'

I drove to the hospital that Saturday morning with my head spinning. Surely in this modern age there was some way of getting round a colotomy? Did the Americans have an answer? What about a small transplant. If a bit of good intestine was all that was lacking they could help themselves to some of mine. Not that the colotomy bothered me. I had told Lillian the truth. I just felt that for a girl so young and active and above all with almost a fetish about cleanliness it would be a terrible burden.

Mr Hawley was waiting for me when I arrived. He ushered me into a room opposite the reception desk and sat facing me across a small coffee table. I was just about to launch into my prepared speech when he exploded the world in my face.

'I'm sorry to have to tell you Lillian is seriously ill.' he said. 'She has a malignant growth.'

Was that him talking? Had he really said what I thought? And if he had, how was it I was still sitting in the same position saying, 'You mean cancer?'

The mouth in front of me moved again. 'Yes. It's a terrible thing for me to have to tell you, but you mustn't plan too much for the future. There's a slim chance we can operate, but it's only a slim chance.'

'And if the operation is successful, how . . . how long?'

'Perhaps three years.'

'And if it's not?'

'Two months, maybe three.'

Suddenly I was aware that I had lit a cigarette and the ash was falling on to my trousers. Something in the back of my mind was screaming, 'All right, I know this sort of thing happens to other people. But it doesn't happen to me.' But he was still talking.

'We only made certain it was cancer after the second biopsy. It spreads very quickly in young people, and the healthier they are the quicker it spreads.'

'What about the diagnosis, Crohn's Disease?'

'They're very similar in the early stages and Lillian's symptoms were in accordance with Crohn's.'

I was finding it a little difficult to breath now. What a terrible, austere room this was. How many other people had sat here and been told the same sort of thing?

'This operation. When will you do it?'

'Next Thursday.'

'Why not this weekend. Why not tomorrow? Why not today, now?'

'It makes little difference at this stage. I'm afraid we're not very hopeful.'

'And Lillian, what does she know . . . and her parents?'

'Lillian knows nothing, but I told her parents a fortnight ago. They asked me to spare you from this for as long as possible.'

'Will you tell Lillian?'

'If she asked me straight out I'd have to.'

Suddenly I had to get out of the room, back to reality. Then I remembered I had promised Lillian I would look in on her once I had seen Mr Hawley.

'I . . . I've got to go and see Lillian,' I told him, standing up on legs which had suddenly gone numb. God, isn't it cold in this room. Don't they have any heaters?

'Perhaps you should walk around outside for a while.'

'No. The shock's going to come in another half hour or so,' I said, wondering how I could be so definite about anything right then. 'I've got to go and see Lillian now, or I'll never face her again.'

'You'll carry on visiting Lillian?'

The question took some seconds to sink in. 'Eh? Of course I will.'

'Good, we were just a little worried how you'd react. You're pretty important to her you know.'

The flight of stairs to Lillian's ward felt like Everest and and I had to stop at the top to get my breath back. One of the nurses saw me. 'You've seen the doctor . . . he's told you . . . ?'

I started to stammer some sort of reply but then I saw that Lillian had noticed me and was waving. She doesn't look any different, I thought stupidly. Then I realised that nothing was different. She had had cancer yesterday, the week before, three months ago. Only now I knew. I walked across to her with a fixed smile.

'Hi, how are you feeling today?'

'Oh, not so bad. Did you see Mr Hawley?'

'Yes, but he couldn't add much to what you told me yesterday. They're thinking of doing an exploratory operation next week to see if they can cure the stricture by surgery, but it doesn't sound much worse than the operation you've already had.'

I thanked God that I'd always been a pretty good liar because I knew in the next few weeks it was going to be my biggest virtue. Lillian was so unsuspecting lying there in a pretty pale green nightdress, her still carefully kept hair, falling gently just above her shoulders.

'You've got a match to do this afternoon, haven't you?' she said. 'Make sure you don't miss your train.'

A match? What match? What day is it? . . . Saturday . . . oh, God, yes. Wolverhampton Wanderers against Manchester United . . . a two-hour train journey and then sit there watching the game and talk to the players afterwards . . . I can't do it . . . what do other people do in this sort of situation . . . surely they couldn't do it?

I said, 'Yes, that's right and I've got to try and get some interviews for a special feature we're running. I'd better get a move on. If I get back in time I'll see you tonight, otherwise I'll be in as usual tomorrow.'

I walked across the ward as slowly and calmly as possible, so intent on doing it normally that I almost forgot to wave as I reached the door. I walked out of the hospital and crossed the road. I turned into a side-street and crossed the road. I turned into a dead-end alley, turned back into the side-street and crossed the road.

Cancer? Lillian? How, why? . . . it was unbelievable, yet I had to believe it or I'd be insane. But hadn't George told me that a psychiatrist friend he'd met in the pub told him you didn't get malignant growths in the rectum? And hadn't that been the reason I'd never, not once, suspected cancer?

Now what? go to the match? Of course not, I told myself, it would be impossible. But where would I go if I didn't? It would bring complications at work and I had to carry on as normally as possible for Lillian's sake. First, because it was an act I'd have to get used to when visiting her. Second, because if a word of her illness leaked out and got back to her it would be tantamount to murder.

So I went. And sat in the train until I could bear it no longer and then stood in the corridor where nobody could see my face. Then I sat at the match and tried to talk to people I knew. It was a dream-world that didn't end until I got home that night and then the pent-up shock and misery came in one terrible flood. When it had passed I was left with an unshakable belief: Lillian would be all right. She had the strength and the courage to beat it. This had been sent to test her, not to destroy her. She was to be an example to others—yes, that was it, she had been singled out to inspire people to beat cancer.

I met Frances and Irene at the hospital two days later during an afternoon visiting session. We went for a cup of tea in a café opposite the hospital. I felt I had to reassure them, make them feel as I did, that it would all be all right. 'Don't worry about this,' I said. 'I just know Lillian will get better.'

'We know,' they said. 'We were going to tell you the same thing.'

They recalled how they had been seen by Mr Hawley and Sir Francis Avery-Jones's deputy, Dr Lennard-Jones, a fortnight earlier.

'I fainted when I visited Lillian the following night,' Irene said. 'I was combing her hair and the next thing I knew I was lying on the floor under the bed.'

'George is a broken man,' Frances said. 'He's having to take pills to sleep and others during the day. But I just *feel* Lillian's going to get better. If there's any justice at all in this world she must get better. I'm praying and praying. I'm doing my housework when I suddenly find I'm on my knees. Surely He must hear me?'

The days dragged slowly towards the following Thursday and Lillian's operation. I saw George, Frances and Irene at several visiting times and after each session we would compare what each of us had told Lillian to make sure our stories tallied and she had no grounds for suspicion.

The Wednesday before the operation I arrived to find Lillian looking distressed. I had an awful fear that she had at last found out, but relaxed as she said, 'I asked the nurse if I'll be able to have children after this operation and she said she didn't know. Oh, wouldn't that be terrible. I couldn't ask you to accept that. I sometimes think I'm ill because I've had a lot of fame and been to lots of nice places and now I'm paying for it. But that wouldn't be right, would it? It would be too high a price to pay.'

Later on I excused myself on the pretence of getting Lillian some fresh water and went in to see the sister. Mr Hawley was there as well.

'She's worried out of her mind,' I told them. 'For goodness sake go in when I've left and tell her she'll be able to have children. That's the last thing she wants to worry about at the moment.'

'I was just being told about it,' Mr Hawley said. 'I'll try to put her mind at rest.'

The following day Lillian was more relaxed. 'Mr Hawley explained that the nurse had only said that because it's impossible to say if anyone is capable of having children,' she said. 'At least that's one worry less.'

Lillian was nervous about the operation, but less so than before the colotomy. 'The only thing I'm scared about is if I wake up and find I've got a permanent colotomy,' she said. 'But at least then I'll know it's all over.'

The operation was scheduled for the afternoon. I saw Mr Hawley just before I left at lunchtime. 'If we can do the operation we'll be in the theatre until the early evening,' he said. 'There's not much point coming back until about six-thirty.'

I decided to spend the next couple of hours in a small church at Petersham, just outside Richmond. I had never been very religious but, on a couple of previous occasions in my life when I had felt the need to pray I had gone to that church. Perhaps I had an affinity with the place because there is a monument there to an uncle of mine who died in the war. I was named after him and to some degree our earlier lives ran on parallel lines. Whenever I had passed the church previously its doors had been opened. That afternoon they were locked and I experienced a moment's panic as I took it to be a sign. But then I read the notice which told me to apply next door for the key. The church stayed deserted until I left just after four-thirty p.m. I went for a walk in nearby Richmond Park and then drove slowly back to the hospital.

I arrived just after six p.m. and was told Mr Hawley was still in the theatre. As the minutes ticked by I grew more and more excited. Remember what he said, I told myself. If they are able to do the operation they will be in the theatre until the evening.

By six forty-five I had made plans to buy Mr Hawley a celebration drink in the pub opposite the hospital. 'I don't care if you never drink,' I could hear myself telling him, 'there's a time when we've all got to let go . . . and as far as I'm concerned that's right now. What was it you wanted? Whisky? Here have a double, just for starters.'

At seven-fifteen I saw him coming down the stairs towards where I sat. As I rose to greet him the look on his face wiped away my expectant smile and the day-dreams of the past half hour mocked me briefly as he opened the door to that all too familiar room.

'I'm sorry, David,' he said. 'It's hopeless. We can do nothing. The cancer is all over her stomach. The spores have come pouring through from a huge tumour in her rectum. I'm afraid it's even worse than we feared.'

The numbness was back again. After a week of building up hope, suddenly there was nothing to hope for. I had crawled to my feet at the count of nine to find my opponent waiting with the k.o. punch.

'How long?'

'About two months, although of course it's hard to be precise.'

'What about these cases of incurable cancer suddenly getting better?' I was desperate now, ready to clutch at any straw he might hand me.

'You sometimes hear of cancer going into spontaneous regression,' he said. 'But no one knows why this happens. We can only pray for a miracle now. But frankly I don't think she'll get out of hospital.'

As I left the hospital I tried to analyse how I felt and the answer surprised me. Upset . . . of course. Shocked . . . a little. Angry . . . angry? Yes, one hundred per cent absolutely bloody raging mad. My Lillian dying of cancer? Too late to operate? Nothing left for it but to pray for miracles and watch her die day by day? Not bloody likely. I would fight with everything I had, and anyway I knew how to get her better. This was war and for the first time in my life I was totally committed to something.

I had broken the news the day before to two of my oldest

friends, Geraldine and Philip Baker, who had married the previous year and were now living near my parents in West Ewell. I called round to see them when I got back from the hospital and they insisted I went with them to see another old friend of ours, Geoff Wootton, whose wife had just given birth to a daughter. It seemed almost macabre to be celebrating a birth at that time, but I felt like company and was too pent up just to sit around doing nothing. So I went with them and the events of the next few hours made me feel it was fate working all over again.

Soon after we reached Geoff's the conversation somehow came round to faith healing. It was nothing to do with me. I had sat there hardly daring to say a word in case I should reveal what had happened and completely ruin what should have been a happy night for Geoff. But there we were discussing what must surely be my first step towards trying everything to help Lillian. I knew Phil had been to a few spiritualist meetings a couple of years earlier and I asked him about it on the way home in the car.

Two nights later, in a pub in Cheam, he introduced me to Eric, a spiritualist healer. Up to that point I had had a few reservations about the idea. But Eric struck me as such a normal, likeable person with a genuine concern about people that I decided I had done the right thing. Eric told me he felt Lillian could be saved but he would know better after a few days. In the meantime, he said he felt a 'transference'. The next afternoon at the hospital the nurses told me that Lillian had been moved to a private room. In my state of mind it was nearly all the proof I needed.

Eric had given me the telephone number of one of the country's top mediums. I rang him at his Lancashire home that evening. 'I feel everything will be all right,' he told me. 'Just trust in Eric and do as he says.'

The next day I happened to look at Lillian's star sign, Sagittarius, in the *Daily Mail*. It said, 'Because of faith in you, people will rely on you to perform miracles. You justify their confidence. Rewarding for you, too.' If I was ready to clutch at straws, then in the past forty-eight hours I had been handed a hay stack. The feeling I had always had that things would turn out all right had now become cast-iron conviction—and it made visiting times so much easier.

These had become something of an ordeal after Lillian's exploratory operation. She lay there so quietly, so deathly white and with hardly the strength to move her head. Every night I was terrified the phone would ring and every day I arrived at the hospital I was scared to look at the face of the first nurse I met on Lillian's floor.

Gradually, to the astonishment of the hospital staff, Lillian won back a little of her strength. After a week she was able to get out of bed to wash. But the first time I saw her standing up I had to turn away to hide the look of shock I could feel contorting my face. She was so thin. In one week since the operation she must have lost one and a half stone. Her legs were the same size as my arms and now she was out of bed I could see the same was true of the rest of her body.

The amazing thing was she had never once asked what had happened during the operation. Every day the nurses and doctors waited for her to ask the questions that would force the answers they dreaded to give. But every day she said nothing. Gradually the truth dawned on me. Lillian believed she had been given a permanent colotomy and that she was now gaining strength simply to go home. If that was the case there was certainly no harm in it; for every day she would strive harder to convince herself she was recovering and without knowing it she would be giving herself the will to live that was so vital. I helped her as much as possible. Ten days after the operation I walked her round the room. The following day I took her into her old ward to see a few of the friends she had made and the next day she walked up and down a flight of stairs.

I had forgotten all about my twenty-fourth birthday on October 13th. But Lillian hadn't. She had continued to wear her make-up every day since recovering from the operation. But that afternoon it was immaculate. She greeted me with a huge smile and pulled a bundle of parcels from under the bed.

'I was so disappointed I couldn't choose your presents myself,' she said. 'But I told Irene what I wanted to get and she's done it all for me.'

There were a black roll-neck sweater, a blue shirt and a bottle of the most expensive after-shave lotion. It was a marvellous surprise and one I should have expected from a girl with her amazing ability always to think of others no matter what she was going through herself. But the sadness of the situation made me desperately unhappy and it was a few seconds before I trusted myself to speak.

'You're wonderful,' I told her. 'These presents are all superb, but you've given me the best one of all just by sitting there looking so perky.'

And there was that fate thing working again. I had always made a lot out of the fact that Lillian and I had both been born on the 13th. It had always been our lucky day—and there she was sitting up in bed on the 13th, as if nothing had happened, just over a week after a nurse had confided to me that she thought Lillian would die in a fortnight.

But it couldn't last. A bout of sickness lasting twenty-four hours wiped out all she had striven for and she was forced to realise she was getting no better.

'I asked them what happened during the operation,' she told me the following day when I arrived, and I could feel my heart sink. 'They told me they were unable to do the operation just yet; that the stricture's still too big. What does it all mean? I'm not just going to lie here and gradually waste away until I die, am I?'

I told her, of course not; that the fact that they hadn't done the operation was a good thing because it meant that she might now recover fully without the need for any more surgery. And in fact that was what I believed. I had convinced myself that fate's reason for not allowing the operation to be possible was because Lillian was due for a full recovery. If the operation had been successful its savagery would have meant that Lillian would have been little more than a shell for the remaining handful of years she had left.

I had been in contact with Eric every couple of days since our first meeting and that night when I telephoned he said he felt he must see Lillian to be able to help her to the full extent of his powers. I said yes, of course, and arranged to take him the next afternoon. But when I put the phone down I realised the problems involved. First, he would have to be introduced in a way that would arouse no suspicion in Lillian's mind. Second, I did not want any of the doctors knowing what was happening in case they would refuse to let Eric in. I was unsure of the law about spiritualist healers.

We arrived at the hospital at three p.m. (Eric having refused money even for petrol). I explained the situation to him, apologised for treating him a bit like a housebreaker, and hid him in the small chapel next to Lillian's room until I was sure no one was about.

Lillian was sitting up in bed as I went in. 'I hope you don't mind,' I told her. 'But I was just coming into the hospital when I met an old friend. It's quite a coincidence really. Someone he knew had to have a colotomy recently and he asked if he could come in to offer you some reassurance, just in case you do ever have to have a permanent one. Apparently his friend has recovered fully now and is doing everything just as before the operation.'

I could feel myself going deeper and deeper into the excuse, but it was impossible to stop in mid-stream. Lillian seemed to accept it all, however, and said: 'Yes, fine. But only for a few minutes.'

Eric came in, and said his piece and then sat there quietly while I chatted to Lillian. He excused himself after a quarter of an hour and waited for me down by the car.

'I still feel something can be done,' he said when I rejoined him. 'But I find it hard to get through to her. I got a tremendous headache just sitting there concentrating. I've got a feeling, though, that if something is going to go wrong it will be centred in her head.'

Eric told me he would continue to do everything he could, personally as well as by saying prayers during the regular Sunday circle meeting.

There was little to do but sit back and wait for something to happen. It did. On Wednesday, October 21st.

'I want to go home,' Lillian told me out of the blue. 'I'm

absolutely sick of this place. I want to get back to my own bedroom even if it's only for a few weeks and then I have to come back here.'

And when I thought of it there was no reason why she shouldn't. I had been so accustomed to thinking that she would have to spend whatever time remained before the 'miracle happened' in hospital that I had never considered her going home.

'Of course you can,' I told her. 'In fact I promise you you'll be out of here by the weekend.'

Lillian asked her parents the same night. 'Are you sure you can cope?' one of the nurses asked Frances.

'Cope? To get Lillian home now she's asked to come back I'd work till I dropped.'

LEARNING THE TRUTH

It had been decided that I would stay at Lillian's house once she came out of hospital. I especially wanted to be close to her, both because time might prove precious—despite my conviction that everything would turn out all right—and in case of emergencies. Lillian, too, was happy for us to be together after those long weeks of snatched hours at the hospital bedside. My staying also meant George and Irene could carry on working. Frances had applied for time off from her job in the Town Hall, so either she or I would be with Lillian during the day. By the time I had to leave for work in the evening the others would be returning home.

On the Saturday Lillian came home—October 24th—I was due to cover a football match at Ipswich. We had decided it was best to carry on as normally as possible so as not to arouse any suspicion in Lillian's mind. So I went, leaving the family to collect her in her brother George's car. I arrived at the house just after seven p.m. to find Lillian's father looking anxious. He ushered me into the living room. 'What's wrong?' I asked. 'Lillian came home all right, didn't she?'

'Yes, she's upstairs in bed,' George said. 'But she's been in terrible pain for the last hour. The hospital gave us pain-killing injections to bring away, but Saturday is the one day our local doctor isn't available in the evenings. We've rung for an emergency doctor, but that was an hour ago.' He sat down on a chair with his head in his hands. 'This was the one thing I was frightened of,' he said. 'That Lillian would come home, be in agony and we could do nothing to help. I honestly don't know if it would be better for her back in hospital.'

Lillian was sitting up in bed as I walked into her room. Her face was drawn and she was clutching her stomach with both hands. But she still managed a smile.

'Oh,' she said. 'That's the first time I've been disappointed to see you. I thought you were the doctor.'

Frances and Irene were in the room trying to carry on conversations to keep Lillian's mind off the pain.

'How was the ride home?' I asked.

'Great,' said Irene. 'She was up, dressed and waiting for us. We were held up on the way there, arrived one minute late and she told us off!'

'I felt as if I had been let out of jail,' Lillian said. 'Driving home was like travelling through a foreign country. I had forgotten what everything looked like.'

'We went past the "Myllet" and she wanted to pop in for a quick one to celebrate,' Irene said. 'But I told her mummy had spent hours getting everything ready at home, so we came straight back.'

But as each conversation failed and there was still no sign of the doctor Lillian grew more and more distressed. I found myself in the same dilemma as George. Lillian would probably be better off physically in hospital, but would it harm her mentally? From the few cases I had heard of people beating cancer I knew it was essential to have a fierce will to live. With Lillian home we could try to keep her reasonably active and interested in things. Every couple of days we could dream up some treat she could look forward to. With her strength of mind and our help perhaps the miracle would happen.

At nine p.m.—after a stream of telephone calls that grew more angry and desperate—Lillian's three-hour ordeal ended. A young doctor arrived, apologised for being held up on a heart case, and administered the injection. It had been a supreme test of Lillian's courage and she had borne it, as always, without complaint. The doctor came back down the stairs visibly moved. It was a reaction we were to see so many times in the weeks ahead. 'Is that *the* Lillian Board?' he asked. 'Goodness, hasn't she lost weight. I never recognised her.'

The injection took effect within twenty minutes. Lillian's whole body relaxed, her face grew fuller and her eyes lost their dullness. She was a new person—or, rather, she was herself again. The crisis had passed and we had six clear days of a regular doctor's service in which to make arrangements for the next Saturday.

Over the next few days life settled into something of a routine. A district nurse called each morning at ten o'clock to give Lillian her first injection and Lillian's G.P., Dr Sidney Abelson, came at ten p.m. for the second. In between Lillian could take a pain-killing solution prepared by the hospital. This medicine—as Lillian called it—did not prove effective, however. And, as she was determined to have injections only if they were essential, she once went eighteen hours without drugs—to the astonishment of Dr Abelson.

Lillian would sleep fairly well after her night injection until about three a.m. Then, if she woke up and was feeling restless we arranged that she was to tap on the wall of the adjoining bedroom where I was sleeping and I would go in and chat until she felt tired again. We were naturally worried about her dreadful loss of weight but with our constant encouragement to her to eat little and often and Frances' careful cooking she regained some of her appetite. Most of all, though, it was the terrible helplessness that weighed heavily on us.

George told me once, 'If they said go out and knock down the Empire State Building and she'll be cured at least you'd feel as if you could do something.' Also we knew we were running out of time. How much longer would the pain-killers prove effective? When would Lillian start to suspect that she was seriously ill? She had trusted the answers we gave up till now, but as her decline continued would she start to probe deeper? In this state of mind we were ready to try anything. So when George came off the phone on Tuesday evening after speaking to Alf Cotton, chief coach

129

of London Olympiades, he moved more purposefully than for a long time.

'Look,' he told us. 'I don't know what you think of this —I don't even know myself. But Alf has just been telling me about a little girl from Guernsey who was supposed to have miraculous healing powers. Her name was Linda Martell and she died at the age of five. But by the time she died she was already an adult mentally. The island legend says she cured hundreds of people—and that cures are still being carried out by people touching parts of her clothing. Alf has a lot of friends on the island because he is their national walking coach. They have spoken to Linda's father and he has sent Alf a piece of clothing. He wants us to meet him tonight and talk about it.'

George and I met Alf and his wife Mabel an hour later in the 'Myllet'. Mabel, usually so cheerful and lively, sat quietly as Alf took an envelope from his pocket and handed it to me.

'I'm the same as you,' he said. 'I don't know if I believe in any of this or not, but anything is worth a try.'

The envelope contained a small piece of cloth about two inches square and a letter from friends of Alf in Guernsey.

By now I was willing to believe in anything that might help. I had taken my mother to our first spiritualist meeting the previous Sunday—and if we were going to try the unknown we might as well try every aspect of it. The only problem was getting Lillian to wear the piece of cloth without making her suspicious. We decided I would give it to Lillian the following day with some dreamt-up explanation. I would tell her her parents knew nothing about it, so if she thought I was mad at least she could confide in them.

I waited until the following afternoon when the effects of Lillian's morning injection were just wearing off. We started talking about pain and the various ways people tried to fight it. Lillian told me she concentrated on music from the radio or tried to get involved in simple tasks like painting her nails. I mentioned I had read about people getting relief from wearing pieces of clothing which had belonged to a little girl from Guernsey—and quickly sketched out the legend Alf had told me.

'It seems a bit far-fetched, I suppose,' I told her. 'But who can be sure if any of these things work or not? It's a bit like wearing copper bracelets to cure arthritis.'

Lillian seemed to be interested in the subject and began to ask a few questions.

'Well, actually,' I told her. 'I've got a bit of this "magic" cloth right here.' I told her a friend of mine who believed in that sort of thing had got it for me, thinking it would help. She laughed as I handed it to her, but she was obviously intrigued. 'Call me nutty if you like,' I said. 'But let's give it a try.' She was sceptical, but agreed.

Coincidence or not, that night her colotomy, which had been constipated for three days, freed itself and the next day was the most comfortable she had known for some time. From then on she wore the piece of cloth twenty-four hours a day before losing it in Germany a couple of weeks before she died.

* * *

Besides trying to nurture Lillian's appetite, we also wanted to keep her as naturally active as possible. In this we were helped by her tremendous will-power and love of the outdoors. After two months cooped up in hospital she was just as anxious as we were that she should get out and about. She decided to do it in stages. On the Monday she came downstairs for a couple of hours. On the Tuesday she walked into the garden. And on Wednesday she asked to go for a car ride. She dressed slowly with the help of Frances and then, as always, meticulously combed her hair and put on her make-up.

It was while watching her sitting engrossed in front of the dressing-table that I realised again what a terrible burden the colotomy must have been to her. For someone so pains-taking about personal cleanliness and with an abhorrence of mess and untidiness, it was one of the cruellest possible handicaps. Finally she was ready and as she turned to see me standing in the doorway where I had been waiting, overcoat on, for the past ten minutes, she smiled. 'Just like old times,' she said. 'But I expect I'm even slower now.'

She moved determinedly down the stairs. But as she reached the bottom she was caught in a sudden gripping pain that bent her almost double. She leaned against the wall and I could see small beads of perspiration running through her make-up. I waited a couple of minutes and then asked, 'Perhaps we should leave it?'

'No we won't,' she answered almost angrily. 'If we only go out when I've got no pain we'll never get out.' She made a supreme effort to straighten herself and strode down the garden path to my car.

I had intended driving only a short distance as it was Lillian's first time out and aimed for a nearby beauty spot at Horsenden Hill. But after we had been out for half an hour and I suggested going home, she looked disappointed.

'Oh, not yet,' she said. 'I'm just starting to enjoy it—and I was thinking of trying a short walk later on.' And so she did, a good fifty yards, and it was with a feeling of accomplishment that we arrived home two hours later.

For the next two days we went out in the car for at least an hour each afternoon. This, plus Lillian's improving appetite—apart from occasional bouts of sickness—made us feel we were making some progress. Certainly it impressed Dr Abelson and the nurses at St Mark's Hospital, whom I saw when I called in to collect some more pain-killing injections. But Lillian's condition deteriorated sharply on the Saturday. She had a bad night and was in constant pain throughout the day. We wondered if some of it might be psychological with Lillian remembering the terrible time she had had the previous Saturday. But whatever the reason we were forced twice to call in Dr Abelson who had gladly given up his free day to be on stand-by for us.

Lillian had set her sights on visiting my parents and sister that Sunday. It seemed obvious I would have to cancel the arrangements—but I reckoned without Lillian's incredible determination, a refusal to accept defeat in anything she had decided to achieve. That afternoon she won what for me will always be one of her greatest battles. Shrugging off the last disastrous forty-eight hours she persuaded me she was well enough to travel, greeted my parents with her usual affection and then forced down one of the biggest meals she had eaten for months. She sat quietly in obvious distress all the afternoon listening to records and watching television, but would not budge to return home until nine p.m. But even her courage could not side-track the cancer's deadly course. Her condition nose-dived and it was in desperation that I remembered the *Observer*'s front page story on Dr Josef Issels' clinic. And that was when coincidence, or what I at the time thought was fate, took over.

On the Tuesday afternoon of Lillian's second week at home I mentioned the clinic to Frances. 'It says the clinic has a seventeen per cent success rate,' I told her. 'Even one per cent is more than we've been given.' But for all the hope it offered there were some terrible drawbacks. Worst of all Lillian would have to know what was wrong with her. Second, it seemed Lillian would have to be separated from her family and third, it would cost about £1,000 for the three-months' treatment. Then, that evening as I sat at work I glanced at the T.V. programmes for the first time in weeks. The B.B.C. had chosen that very night to show their film on the clinic. I telephoned George and asked him to watch it.

When I arrived home after work we discussed the programme but reached deadlock. Frances and I were set to clutch at any straw. George and Irene were against the idea because of its savage implications. The one fact that had swayed the balance for me was that doctors at St Mark's had told me Lillian would probably find out eventually what was wrong with her. She was certain to start asking un-answerable questions some time. At least if we told her now we would be offering a possible cure. And for her sake we could make her condition out to be less serious than it was and tell her the clinic was 'the most exclusive and successful in the world'.

I wrestled with the problem all day Wednesday and by

Thursday—Guy Fawkes Night—had gone round in so many circles that I was ready to drop the whole idea. But that afternoon I called in on my parents while I was out buying fireworks and sausages for a firework party for Lillian. I explained the situation to my mother.

'Why don't you contact the clinic?' she said. 'If there's a huge waiting list you'll know its pointless trying to do anything anyway.'

First I had to find the telephone number, so I rang Sir Francis Avery-Jones, thinking that as a specialist he might have some knowledge of Dr Issels. But he couldn't help. 'I can give you no encouragement at all,' he told me. 'There's a few of these clinics around, but I don't know much about them. I feel patients are far better left in their own environment.'

'But in her own environment what chance does Lillian stand?' I asked him.

He paused. 'None at all, I'm afraid.'

'Then surely a possible seventeen per cent chance is better than nothing?'

He repeated, 'I can't help you at all. Why don't you contact the B.B.C. They showed the film didn't they?'

So I did and their Press Office gave me the number immediately. I rang it and was amazed to get an answer from a woman speaking almost perfect English. I tried to tell her the situation without mentioning names. 'Can she walk?' she asked. 'Oh, that's good. Yes, we have a bed available—when can you come, tomorrow?'

I was almost bursting with news as I returned to Lillian's house. But Lillian was downstairs in her dressing gown waiting for the fireworks and I did not have a chance to talk to anybody until the party ended about an hour later. Lillian was disappointed when it was over. She had eaten about six sausages and shown more genuine interest than for about a week.

George and I drove to the 'Myllet' so I could explain what had happened in private. He was still understandably reluctant until Bill Fisher, his friend for years and one of Lillian's greatest fans, stepped in. He had listened quietly to the whole thing. 'I only want to ask one thing, George,' he said. 'What time's the plane? I think you must give Lillian every possible chance. You'll hate yourself in years to come if Lillian doesn't get better and you start to wonder what would have happened if you had tried this clinic.'

When we got home I discussed the situation with Irene, and she, too, agreed it would be for the best. 'I suppose I was being selfish,' she said. 'I just couldn't bear the thought of Lillian being miles away from us in case anything should happen.'

It was decided I would collect Lillian's medical dossier, pick up the air tickets, arrange for time off work, and try to raise the money the following day. Once everything was finalised I would tell Lillian she had cancer. It was one of the busiest days in my life, but in a funny way it was one of the happiest. Something tangible was being done to help Lillian.

By four-thirty p.m. the arrangements were complete. Lillian's surgeon at St Mark's, Mr Peter Hawley, had gone out of his way to be helpful. He gathered together Lillian's medical history, cleared her for flying at the airport and told me not to hesitate to call if I needed any more information once we reached Germany. 'I know you realise just how seriously ill she is,' he said. 'And this must be the slimmest of slim chances. But I can understand you wanting to try it.'

As I travelled back to Lillian's house I began to think about the full extent of what I was about to tell her. Everything had been moving so fast up until then that I had had no time to be nervous. Now I felt really sick as I wondered how she would take it. I thought I knew her well enough to be sure that she would be willing to fight; that she would believe me when I told her she was going to get better. I tried to work out my opening sentence a dozen times, but I stopped short as soon as I came to the word cancer.

Lilling was reading as I went into her bedroom and looked happy to see me. An awful feeling waved over me that it might be the last time. She was like a vulnerable little girl sitting there and I was about to shatter her life. But it was no good hesitating or I would never do it. 'How are you feeling?' I asked.

'The pain's pretty bad,' she said. 'Where have you been all day?'

'I had a few people I had to see in London and I called in for a chat with Mr Hawley . . . Look, have you ever wondered if your illness might be a little bit more serious than you think?'

'What do you mean?' Lillian asked. But I paused too long. 'Oh, come on, what do you mean? Tell me, you're frightening me.'

I had a sudden moment of panic as I realised I had probably made a mess of things. But was there any gentle way of saying what I had to say?

'No, no, it's all right,' I told her. 'Don't worry, you're going to be all right. It's just that it's not Crohn's Disease you've got but a mild form of cancer—and its only mild,' I finished in a rush.

'Cancer,' she gasped in a split second of hysteria. 'Oh, no!'

I thanked God as Frances walked in at that moment. She had been waiting just outside. 'Lillian,' she said firmly, 'you're going to be all right. Listen to what else David has to tell you.'

'Yes,' I said. 'The only reason I'm telling you this is because we've got you booked in at a clinic that will cure you. You'd probably get better over here anyway, but in this place it will be much quicker.'

Lillian had recovered from her shock now and I could see that a few things which had been puzzling her over the past months were falling into place.

'Where is this clinic?' she asked at last.

'In the Bavarian Alps near Munich,' I told her.

'I can't go all the way over there by myself?'

'No, I'm coming with you. I've arranged to have all the time off work I need until you're well again. And when you are well we can stay on for a holiday.'

She relaxed. 'It'll be a bit like the skiing holiday we've been planning,' she said. 'I'd better work out what I'll have to take in the way of clothes.'

136

12

THE RINGBERG CLINIC

Lillian was awake early the next morning and seemed almost eager to get started. My fears that the knowledge of what was wrong with her might have weighed heavily during the night were dispelled as soon as I saw her. She was cheerfully organising the last of her packing with Frances and Irene, carefully picking out most of her warmer clothes for the Bavarian winter.

'I'm going to need a pair of boots,' she told me as I looked into her room. 'Mine are much too big now and there's bound to be a lot of snow over there.'

'We'll buy some when we arrive,' I said. 'They make some beautiful snow boots in Germany.'

But she was hardly listening to my reply as she watched Frances rummage through her wardrobe. 'Yes, I'd better take that, no that can stay. Oh, and I'll probably need those shoes as well.'

It was a routine she had been through so many times before when preparing for athletic trips. This familiarity plus the fact that her luggage was Mexico Olympic issue, embossed with the Olympic symbol of five linked rings, made me feel for a moment that the last three months had just been part of an awful nightmare . . . that Lillian was simply getting ready for another athletic international. But in the split-second the illusion occurred to me Lillian turned and said, 'Do you know, this is the first time for six years that I've been getting ready to go away without having to take any running gear with me? Usually half my suitcase is taken up with track suits, running clothes, spikes and starting blocks.'

In a way the thought seemed to please her. She was to tell me later, 'One of the things I looked forward to when we were planning a holiday before I was ill was that we could drive somewhere or fly off without me knowing that when we arrived I was going to compete, with all the nerves and tension that entailed. It would have been a marvellous sense of freedom.'

But even on that Saturday morning of November 7th as we prepared to fly out to what many were to describe as Lillian's greatest race, she looked relaxed and happy. It was almost as if knowing what was wrong with her had removed a deep subconscious block. She had recognised her enemy and had the strength of mind to face it. And, like me, she was confident she could beat it.

She decided to travel in what had become her favourite outfit since coming out of hospital: a tartan skirt, black roll-neck sweater and big fun-fur overcoat. It had been an ensemble she had liked to wear even before she was ill, and it still fitted fairly well. This had partly softened her great disappointment when she found most of her carefully chosen wardrobe was unwearable because of her thinness and the gradual swelling of her stomach.

We were due to catch the ten-forty a.m. plane from Heathrow Airport to Munich. Lillian's brother George drove us there in his large, automatic Zodiac, the most comfortable car we owned. Bill Fisher and Lillian's father would travel behind, both to say goodbye at the Airport and just in case anything went wrong with George's car. Now all the decisions had been made we wanted to get to Germany as fast as possible and with every conceivable hitch covered.

We all gathered in the living room while Lillian finished getting ready with Frances. None of us were in the mood for talking, but from the few words that were spoken I could feel that everyone realised this was the most crucial journey they would witness. I was nervous, but only in anticipation of what we would find when we arrived. The impression I had was of a secluded, castle-like hospital, miles from anywhere and surrounded on all sides by towering mountains. In my imagination I could hear the giant iron gates crashing shut behind us as we entered and the stony-faced authoritarian German matron welcoming Lillian and showing her to a Spartan room, furnished only by a bed and a wash-basin.

But even if that was the case I was still sure we had made the right decision. It was our last possible chance, barring miracles, and we had to take it. Also I was utterly convinced Lillian was destined to be cured in this far-away clinic. Otherwise what was the purpose of our having met the previous January, only a few weeks before the start of the cancer? I felt partially as if fate had sent us together so I could try to give her comfort and strength as she fought for her life.

It was Irene who broke into my day-dream. 'You will telephone us tonight, won't you?' she asked.

'Yes, of course, as soon as Lillian's settled in. And then I'll phone every couple of days until you all come out to see her in a couple of weeks' time.'

I went up the stairs to see how close Lillian was to being ready. As I walked into her room I felt again the almost selfish relief that she now knew what was wrong with her. There was no longer need for lies and deceit; we could talk openly, without secrets, as we always had.

She was titivating in front of the mirror. 'You'll have to get a bit of a move on or we'll be late,' I told her and then felt a little guilty. It sounded as if I seemed to think of this trip as no more than an outing to a dinner party. I had spent so many weeks trying to be casual when talking to her so as not to give any cause for alarm that I found it difficult to break the habit. But she didn't notice. 'I won't be long,' she said. 'I've just got to finish my make-up.' That, as usual, was sooner said than done. Lillian's finishing touches lasted a full thirty minutes and we eventually found ourselves ready to leave fifteen minutes behind schedule. Even so, the delay was reassuring: no matter what shock Lillian had received the previous night, she was now as calm and painstaking as ever.

Dr Abelson had called early in the morning to give Lillian an injection and she carried a second in her handbag in case the effects should wear off during the journey. Frances and Irene said goodbye at the house, frightened that long farewells at the airport might be a strain on Lillian. 'Now don't worry,' Lillian told them, reversing roles from the night before. 'I'm going to be all right.'

I was glad to leave the house, for I was worried that a crowd of reporters might turn up at any time. I knew that once the newspapers realised Lillian knew what was wrong with her they would break the silence they had maintained so magnificently over the past few weeks. For me, the way in which the Press refused to breathe even a hint of Lillian's condition in all that time is the complete answer to anyone who ever questions their integrity.

We were just setting off when what looked like a staff car from one of the Sunday newspapers turned into Lillian's road. But by the time the driver realised what was happening we were a couple of miles away and heading for the airport.

Charles Wilson, Sports Editor of the *Daily Mail*, had arranged for us to be met at the airport by B.E.A. officials so that we could pass quickly through embarkation with the minimum of red tape. While one official was dealing with our passports and boarding cards another came across to me. 'Do you want the dog-cage?' he asked, and then saw the look on my face and added hurriedly, 'I'm sorry, I mean the wheelchair.' It was a harmless enough remark, but the anger it evoked made me realise I was a lot more keyed up than I had let myself believe.

'Hold on and I'll tell you,' I said brusquely, and moved over to where Lillian was saying goodbye to her brother and father.

'There's a wheelchair ready if you want it, honey,' I told her. 'It will probably be quite a long walk to the plane.'

'No, it's all right thanks,' Lillian said. 'I'm not going to be wheeled through here for people to stare at. I'll walk there if you promise to hold me up one side.'

We must have covered a full hundred and fifty yards before we reached the aircraft—treble what Lillian had managed the previous week when she was that much stronger. But she didn't falter once and I had a tremendous feeling of pride as we strolled along almost unnoticed by the rest of the passengers. If it wasn't for the thinness of her legs and the paleness of her face, I thought, no one here would know she was ill. And by the hospital's reckoning she now had about a month to live.

It was a feeling that grew even stronger as we took our seats. 'Any pain?' I asked.

'No, I'm fine. I wonder what we'll get to eat during the flight.'

It was as if we had turned the clock back five months. Certainly she was more subdued than she had been before she was ill and she moved her hands and body more slowly in anything she did. But there was a vitality back in her face; the air of adventure and interest I hadn't seen for a long time.

As the plane took off I had one last, long look at London. 'We'll be back here in three months,' I vowed to myself, 'and the whole of bloody Fleet Street will be waiting as we walk down that gangway hand in hand. And you can go out and win as many more medals as you want but it won't matter a damn to either of us because we'll look back on this as the most important chapter of our lives. This is the beginning of the beginning.'

The flight went smoothly apart from one anxious moment when the air hostesses brought round the morning papers. I could see Lillian's name screaming from every front page and was scared she might read one of the stories and realise she was more ill than we had told her. 'There's no point having a paper,' I said hurriedly as the hostess drew near to us. 'We know more about this than any of the newspaper reporters and they'll probably be guessing at some of the details.' But I needn't have worried. 'I don't want to read them anyway,' Lillian said, showing her usual disinterest in publicity which was really an embarrassment at reading about herself in front of others. 'But it is a bit strange sitting here watching everybody reading about us, and probably none of them realising who we are.'

We were met at Munich Airport by a B.E.A. steward and stewardess. Both spoke perfect English, which was just as well. My 'O' level German was virtually non-existent by now. They told us the car journey to Rottach-Egern would take up to one and a half hours, depending on traffic. We decided Lillian should have half of her spare injection as a safeguard and she was taken to the airport medical centre while we waited for B.E.A. to phone for a car.

For some reason I was expecting everyone in Germany to have heard of the Ringberg Cancer Clinic and it came as a bit of a surprise when the driver of the hire car knew nothing about it. In fact he was even a bit hazy over the location of Rottach-Egern. But Lillian took it all in her stride. 'It's probably because its exclusive, as you said,' she told me, and I found it was now she who was reassuring me. 'It's funny,' she added as the car moved into the dense Munich traffic, 'I feel just like I do before a big race. I want to get there to see what it's like and I know it's something I've got to do. But I want to put it off for as long as possible.'

On the outskirts of Munich we picked up the Salzburg Autobahn and began to make good speed towards the Bavarian Alps. As we sped through the dull, grey afternoon, past the unfamiliar signposts and road-side forests, I experienced again the feeling of unreality. Surely this was all part of a film plot; just sit back and let the actors say their lines and everything will be all right in half an hour's time when we reach the last reel. But a sideways glance at Lillian's poor little, pale face and the feeling of her hand so cold in mine told me this was no make-believe. It was *too* real, *too* immediate. For God's sake let's hurry up and get to that last reel, let's get these three months over, let's see Lillian better. For surely, she more than anyone was never meant to suffer like this.

After fifteen minutes on the Autobahn we had passed from woodland to pastureland. The remnants of a war-time aerodrome arrived and went along with a couple of herds of tatty-looking cows and miles of beautiful rolling grass slopes, dotted here and there with picturesque wooden houses and chateaux. Then, as we came round a long sweep in the road we saw the Alps for the first time, closer than I had thought and with their forbidding peaks covered in mist and snow. We moved off the Autobahn on to the country roads which ran to Bad Tolz and Tegernsee.

Lillian had said little during the journey, but she was now clearly impressed by the panorama that was spread before us. 'It's magnificent,' she said, 'and a bit frightening. Everywhere's so clean and fresh . . . if only we were really coming here for a holiday.'

From the impressions I had been given of the remoteness of the clinic I was still waiting for the driver to turn on to some obscure mountain road when he suddenly pulled up in the main street of a pretty little tourist town. 'This is Rottach-Egern,' he told us, and then, after asking a passer-by, added, 'The clinic is down the next road.' We turned into a badly-made side-road, crossed a small stream and swung into an immaculate gravel drive-way between two gleaming white walls.

At first I thought he had made a mistake, but the sign on the entrance proved him right. We had arrived—and the contrast to what I had expected was so great that I almost shouted with relief. Far from dingy brick walls and high iron gates as I had imagined, the clinic stretched before us like a holiday camp for aristocrats. A large chateau stood resplendent in the middle of the palatial grounds, a picture-postcard building of white walls and polished wood. To one side and at the back I could see smaller houses of the same architectural design, and on all sides there stretched well-kept lawns and gardens.

We drove slowly towards the main house, passing several patients on the way. Some were walking quite briskly, others were being supported by relatives and friends. But in all their faces I thought I could see a look of determination. 'This is all part of the therapy I was telling you about,' I said to Lillian. 'Dr Issels likes his patients to keep as active as possible.'

We pulled up beside the main entrance and were just starting to climb the short flight of steps towards the front door when a cherubic-looking blonde woman in her late forties came hurrying towards us.

'Miss Board? Oh, you have got here quickly,' she said in broken English. 'We did not think you would arrive until tomorrow. But no matter, your bed is ready. I am Frau Margot Findeisen, Dr Issels' sister. Please excuse me, but the doctor is not here today. He had to go to a conference in Baden-Baden. He hoped to be back by the time you arrived.'

Lillian stumbled slightly against one of the steps as we moved towards the reception hall.

'Are you sure you can walk all right?' Mrs Findeisen asked anxiously. 'I have put you in House Diana, one of the outhouses, but perhaps you would be better in the main house which is for patients who are not so active.'

'No, it's all right,' Lillian said. 'I'm just a little tired from travelling.'

Mrs Findeisen looked relieved but continued to bustle around busily making sure Lillian was happy with every detail of the room she was to stay in. 'It is a private room,' she said. 'I though you might not want to share. I'm afraid there is no telephone inside but there is one right outside in the corridor.' Her genuine concern and friendliness again came as a pleasant contrast to what I had expected. It was more like a hotel manager welcoming a guest than a hospital official admitting a patient.

We returned to the car and drove the hundred and fifty yards to House Diana—the fifth and newest of the clinic's 'wards'. Lillian's room was on the first floor of the three-floor building. Mrs Findeisen gave us a quick tour of inspection. Downstairs was the nurses' duty room, a kitchen, a television lounge and the doctor's quarters. The clinic had five doctors besides Dr Issels, one for each house. Lillian would be with Dr Manfred Rosa. Everywhere was spotless. The wooden contemporary furniture gleamed with polish and the white plaster walls looked freshly painted.

Lillian's room measured about 20 ft by 15 ft. A modern

Wearing a pink coat she made herself, Lillian poses for photographers outside Buckingham Palace with her M.B.E., 1970.

A pause in training for what was to be her last race, *(below)* The W.A.A.A. Championships at Crystal Palace, June, 1970; Sheila Carey leads Lillian in staggered lanes in the 800 m. final.

Off the track, two informal moments: Lillian (*above*) enjoys a cuppa with the men laying the tartan track of Crystal Palace. (*Below*) An evening out with the family at the Myllet Arms, Perivale.

Lillian kicks off at a charity soccer match. Her style is being admired by (*from the left*) Terry Downes, Terry Spinks, Judo Al Hayes and Geoff Hurst.

A family joke off the track.

A happy moment with David.

Lillian keeping up with the sporting scene from her bed.

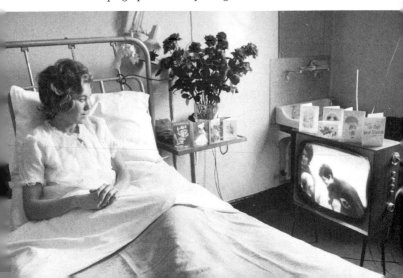

Lillian and the author out shopping near Dr Issels' Clinic with
Frau Melle, the Clinic supervisor.

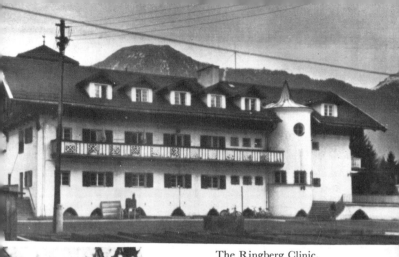

The Ringberg Clinic.

The author (*left*) waiting for news in the grounds of the Clinic; and (*below*) talking to Dr Issels.

A memorial service for Lillian was held at St Paul's Cathedral in January, 1971, when famous faces mingled with the general public paying tribute to the golden girl of British athletics.
(*Above*) Della James with, left and right, family friends Molly and Philip Vivian;
(*right*) Henry Cooper.

divan lay just in front of a large double window which led on to a small private balcony. A grey carpet covered most of the floor and around its edges stood a wardrobe, writing table and chair, bedside table and washbasin. The view from her window looked across a few tall trees at the back of the clinic towards the Austrian Alps in the distance. The only problem left now was to arrange visiting times and I was ready for an argument if these were too short.

'I will be staying in Rottach-Egern,' I told Mrs Findeisen. 'When will I be able to visit?'

'You can come at eight o'clock in the morning,' she said. 'But I'm afraid you will have to leave by nine.'

'What, only one hour?'

'Oh no, nine at night. The patients have to go to sleep then.'

Lillian had just settled in bed and was watching me unpack her suitcases when a tall, regal woman of about forty came into the room. Her face was sternly Germanic and beautiful, compelling attention and exuding authority. She wore a long white leather coat—in a style that reminded me of Second World War Stormtroopers—and knee-length black boots. 'I am Dr Freda,' she said in clipped, military tones, 'I am the Number Two here. I wish to welcome you on behalf of Dr Issels.' It was all a little awe-inspiring, but Lillian's knack of disarming people with sincere straightforwardness bridged the gulf.

'I do like your coat,' she said. 'And your English is excellent.'

'Do you think so?' Dr Freda said, obviously pleased and relaxing her stance. 'I am trying so hard to speak English. I would like some time to go to England to work.' She sat on the edge of the bed. 'But now, if you please, I would like to examine you.' She ran her fingers expertly over Lillian's stomach, inspected her tongue and throat and asked a few questions about her condition over the past few weeks. 'Good,' she said at last. 'You are better than I thought you would be.'

I had had no time to arrange accommodation in Rottach-Egern before we left London. But the clinic quickly took care of that and seemed delighted that I was able to stay with Lillian for the full three months. I left Lillian to rest and took a taxi to my new lodgings which turned out to be a private chalet at the back of a guest house called Haus Lipp, little more than three hundred yards from the clinic. I was in the process of discussing terms with my landlady when a woman and a young man walked into the room. I was surprised when they spoke to me in perfect English.

'Have you just arrived at the clinic with your very famous girl friend?' the woman asked. 'Oh, wonderful. I'm sure you've done the right thing. We heard about Lillian coming and have been waiting for you to turn up. I'm Angela Fox and this is my son Edward. My husband Robin is a patient at the clinic as well.' Mr Fox turned out to be Robin Fox, one of the world's leading theatrical agents. He had arrived at the clinic a few days earlier and up to then was the only English person there.

Mrs Fox and Edward invited me to share supper with them and immediately made me feel at home. They listened without interruption as I ran through the events of the last forty-eight hours, realising probably that I needed an audience to get everything off my chest and unwind. They outlined their story afterwards and then together we discussed the clinic and our first impressions. As we talked I felt for the first time the great sense of comradeship that existed between people connected with the clinic. It was the same bond of pulling together for the lives of loved ones that must have been found in war-time London—and ironically, here we were in the heart of Germany.

Lillian was dozing peacefully when I returned to the clinic. She had eaten a good meal of omelette and salad and was just starting to feel the effects of a sleeping injection. I sat with her until she was asleep and then left to telephone George and Frances. They were relieved and delighted with the smoothness of our trip and my praise for the clinic. When I rang off I knew that, like me, they had mentally wiped out the past few months. We were entering a new era—and it was filled with hope.

I arrived at the clinic at eight a.m. the next morning to

find Lillian sitting up in bed, her make-up on and her hair freshly combed.

'You're awake early, aren't you?'

'Early? I've been ready since seven o'clock. They wake you up at six-thirty.'

She had slept fairly well and eaten a good breakfast. A pretty blonde nurse who introduced herself in good English as Heidi, the station sister of Haus Diana, followed me into the room and explained Lillian's morning routine. With my help she was to take her own pulse, temperature and weight. Also I had to chart everything she ate and drank. She was to have at least 2,000 c.c.s of liquid a day and there were strict rules on diet. No coffee, milk or alcohol—only the spring water that was piped into every room or herbal tea. No sugary food of any kind and fruit only in moderation.

The do-it-yourself aspect surprised me, but then, I told myself, this is a clinic, not a hospital, and the routine is probably designed to keep the patient totally involved with the fight to survive. The diet, I knew, would be hard for Lillian, both because she had always drunk very little—and often only milk—and because of her love of sweet things.

The day passed quietly until the mid-afternoon when Lillian started to become very restless. She was alternately hot and cold and started to perspire heavily. I grew more and more worried until I suddenly realised she was suffering from withdrawal symptoms. For the past two months she had been used to having massive doses of pain-killing dia-morphine, doses so strong that they were almost neat heroin. Since the previous afternoon she had had none at all.

I asked a nurse to find Dr Freda and she came immediately. 'Too much morphine is bad,' she said. 'It poisons the blood. I can give you a little now but you must try gradually to stop taking it.' Lillian slept after the injection but the effects of withdrawal started again that evening with more intensity. Lillian realised she had to beat the craving and endured the awful sensation for another two hours before asking for a second small injection. She had won the major battle, though, for she had morphine only rarely after that during the remaining seven weeks—and then only for severe pain.

An hour after the injection, as Lillian sat reading the first of what was to become a flood of telegrams, we heard sounds of commotion from downstairs. People were scurrying about and the nurses were calling quick orders to one another. I was just moving to see what was happening when a herd of footsteps sounded on the stairway and along the corridor and Lillian's door was flung open.

Dr Issels, surrounded by an entourage of nurses and medical secretaries, strode into the room. He was about 6 ft 1 in and 13 stone, an immaculate, commanding figure, in white, from the greying blondness of his hair to the blancoed tips of his shoes. I could see an immediate resemblance to his sister, Mrs Findeisen. He, too, had the rounded, almost cherubic face which exuded health. But his piercing blue eyes, friendly now, had a steely coldness of determination. I had been told he was sixty-three, but he moved with such agility and sense of purpose that he could have been twenty years younger.

'Ah, Miss Board,' he said.

'Call me Lillian,' she told him at once, bringing everything crashing back to life-size.

'I knew an athlete was coming,' Dr Issels said 'But I did not know she would be world famous. All day long at my conference the reporters were ringing up. All this publicity, all the questions I am asked, how will I ever find time to do my work? But now you are here and now we will make you better so that you can run once more.

'You know I can make you better? You believe it? Good. Together we will fight. You and me. Together we will beat the cancer. Tomorrow he will know we are coming to fight him when we start the treatment. He will feel the strength of our forces. We will have no secrets. Always I will tell you what I am doing and why. Do you trust me? Will you fight with me?'

'Yes,' Lillian told him quietly. 'I am sure you can make me well.'

DR ISSELS

Lillian was dressed and sitting at her bedside table eating breakfast when I arrived the following morning.

'You're up early,' I told her. 'How do you feel?'

'Fine. I slept well and funnily enough I haven't felt any pain this morning so far . . . and I've had no injections. I would have been happy to have stayed in bed a bit longer, but I've got to go over to the main house for a dental inspection and X-rays.'

We walked slowly through the grounds together and I was surprised to find Lillian moving with a little more spring and not holding quite so tightly on to my arm for support. It seemed like an overnight improvement and although I realised it had to be purely psychological at this stage it did wonders for my own morale. For I was sure that Lillian's mental state would be as important as her physical strength if she were to win this battle.

I sat in the main reception room as Lillian went in for her various tests. After a few minutes I recognised one of my fellow guests at my boarding house . . . a middle-aged Austrian woman who spoke fairly good English. She saw me, too, and came over.

'I didn't realise you were connected with the clinic,' I told her.

'You will find that almost everybody at Haus Lipp has relatives here,' she said. 'I am with my brother-in-law.'

'How is he?' I asked.

'He is not good. He has it in the liver and I do not think he will live.'

Her flat statement brought me sharply back to earth. From the time we had arrived I had convinced myself Lillian was half-way to being cured. Now, suddenly, the situation was put back in perspective. But my new neighbour must have sensed my disappointment at her answer.

'Believe me, though,' she said, 'there is hope here. My brother-in-law first came here a year and a half ago. He was given only a few weeks to live. Dr Issels gave us another wonderful year together as a family. But now I fear it is too late.'

I noticed Lillian coming down the main corridor with one of the nurses and stood up to meet her. The Austrian woman went to leave and then turned. 'Really,' she said quietly, 'there is great hope here.'

Lillian separated herself from the nurse and linked her arm through mine. 'I've got to have two front teeth and my tonsils out,' she announced breezily

'Why's that?'

'Oh, it's all part of the therapy apparently. Dr Issels believes bad teeth and tonsils can spread infection. Anyway, after the operations I've had it will seem like nothing.'

I wondered at first if she was just putting on a brave face for my benefit. But when I watched her closely it was obvious she wasn't giving it a second thought and I realised that after the weeks of constant pain this new development was, to her, completely trivial.

Lillian had a short rest while I went shopping in the nearby town for nightdresses. None of Lillian's were allowed in the clinic because they were nylon. Dr Issels insisted on everything being as natural as possible—and that meant cotton night wear. I had a bit of difficulty and a lot more embarrassment through my broken German before I eventually bought what I wanted. They were hardly the latest fashion and I had to settle for a large size, but Lillian seemed happy enough. 'At least they'll keep me warm,' she said, as she wrapped one of them around her twice.

Lillian was still feeling well in the afternoon and decided

she would like to go for a car ride. We hired a taxi and headed through the mountains towards the border road between Germany and Austria. The driver, Irvine, spoke almost fluent English thanks to a love of Western comics and was also a keen sportsman. He recognised Lillian from stories in the local papers and they were soon engrossed in a discussion on athletics.

As we drove slowly through the beautiful scenery of towering firs dwarfed by massive, snow-covered mountains, I could feel the tension of the past two months draining from me. With Lillian chatting happily by my side and looking intently at everything Irvine pointed out along the route, it was impossible to remember those bleak hours of visiting at St Mark's Hospital. Everything was obliterated by an uplifting feeling of hope. We had entered a new era that was a million times farther away from London than an hour and a half plane ride. Perhaps it was a dangerous feeling of security, perhaps I was trying hard to fool myself that everything was fine . . . but whatever the wrongs and rights of my way of thinking the outcome was that my frame of mind was happier than for a long time and this, in part, transferred to Lillian.

That evening Dr Issels called together all the patients and staff for a lecture in the main dining-hall. Every patient who was fit enough to walk attended and by the time Lillian and I arrived there were about three hundred people in the hall. The talk was in German, so we could understand very little. But a show of slides was self-explanatory. Before and after pictures of patients who had been to the clinic and been treated successfully. There were hundreds of them, many of whom had been given only weeks to live when arriving at the clinic. The difference in some of the cases before and after the therapy was so marked that it brought gasps of approval from the audience. I watched with growing delight. If Dr Issels could do this for those people, surely he could do the same for Lillian?

Lillian settled happily in bed afterwards, tired from the car journey and her several short walks. I left when she was asleep and joined Dr Issels who was giving a small staff party in a nearby wine-house. He saw me coming through the door and motioned for me to sit next to him. He seemed genuinely to like me and in return I felt he was a man I could respect as much as any I had met.

I had come to learn a little of Dr Issels' past from chats with other patients and the staff—and it read almost like an adventure from *Boys' Own Paper*. At the outbreak of the war, he had been pushed to the Russian front for treating British wounded at Dunkirk. He had somehow survived while those around him died in their thousands and had eventually returned to Germany. At the end of the war he had been given a job serving in an Allied NAAFI until someone discovered he was a doctor and moved him over to help the medical corps. When he left he had begun his investigation into cancer, a subject which had always fascinated him. He developed his own theories and practised them on a single millionaire patient. The results were successful and the grateful patient donated enough money for Dr Issels to open his clinic at Rottach-Egern. It had snowballed from there until in 1961 he was charged with manslaughter, found guilty and jailed. He appealed and the German Federal Court ordered a re-trial. Dr Issels was released after several weeks' imprisonment, but it was not until 1964 that his appeal was heard and he was cleared.

The case against him was that he had refused to allow four patients to have surgery and they had subsequently died. Issels maintained that he had not only advised them to have surgery, but had told them they stood the risk of death unless they did. The entire business had meant the closure of his clinic for almost four years and left him with a deep dislike of conventional German medicos who had pushed for the charges to be brought. 'They did not understand my work,' he told me later. 'They still don't want to understand.'

But it was not only my company he wanted that evening in the wine-house and after a couple of glasses of wine he switched the conversation to Lillian. 'You know, of course, David, that this is a very serious case. Some of my doctors advised me against taking Lillian. They said, "She is world

famous. If you do not succeed it will ruin your reputation."
But I would not listen to them. I said, "This is a girl who
needs my help. She is a fighter. Perhaps it is an impossible
case. But if we fight together perhaps it is possible."'

I felt a momentary emptiness in my stomach. But then I
told myself, 'He is only saying what you were already told in
England. You know it's serious. But at least he's saying
there is a chance . . . and he has agreed to treat her.' Dr
Issels interrupted my thoughts. 'One other thing, David. If
I tell Lillian to do something she must never say "I will try!"
She must say "I will do it." Then we have a chance . . . yes,
we have a chance.'

'A chance' . . . that was all we had asked from the start.
Now it was up to Lillian to give Dr Issels all the help she
could.

Dr Issels made an early call on Lillian the next morning
and was delighted with her appearance. He turned to leave
after a thorough inspection and then added as if as an after-
thought, 'I have decided to treat you free. Every couple of
months I take on two or three patients for nothing and I
want you to be one of them. My accountants say I am mad,
but it is what I want to do. I have always loved athletics and
was gymnastics champion of West Germany once. This is
my way of repaying many years of happiness.' I had barely
time to gabble out my thanks before he had strode out of the
door to visit the next patient.

Lillian was then taken off to visit the dentist while I gave
her medical history to her house doctor, Dr Rosa. When we
had finished he told me: 'Yesterday's X-rays are good.
Perhaps it is not quite so hopeless as we first thought.' It was
all the encouragement I needed and it must have shown on
my face. 'You look happy,' Lillian told me as best she could
with the handicap of two missing front teeth. 'And I'm
happy, too. Do you know, I've had no pain since I've been
here. I can't understand it. Let's go for another car ride and
have a walk in the mountains. I feel I could walk five miles.'

We spent another pleasant afternoon with Irvine and
walked for almost half a mile before Lillian felt the first
signs of tiredness.

'I just know I'm going to get better,' Lillian told me as we drove back to the clinic. 'It's not very easy having to drink three litres a day, but I'm going to do it and gradually I'll get used to it.'

Everything was going so well I was almost frightened. But then I felt selfish as I thought of George, Frances and Irene waiting anxiously for news back in England.

'I told your parents I would ring them tonight,' I said to Lillian. 'But why don't you speak to them instead? It will be a wonderful surprise.'

'I do miss them,' Lillian said. 'I've been thinking about what they must have gone through when they were told what I had . . . and then all those weeks they kept it secret from me. I don't know how they did it.'

George and I had arranged that the family would come out to Germany after we had been there for a fortnight. But with Lillian so obviously anxious to see them I felt it would be wonderful for everybody if they could make it that coming weekend. I put the idea to Lillian. 'Oh, that would be marvellous,' she said. 'I'll ask them tonight on the phone.'

Lillian's parents were overjoyed to hear her. But it was an emotional reunion for Lillian and I had to break in quietly once. 'Try not to sound too upset or they might start to worry.' Lillian nodded that she had understood, and, bravely keeping the tears from her voice, reassured her parents that the clinic was all we had hoped it would be. Eventually she passed the phone over to me and I arranged with George that he, Frances, Irene and my mother would come out the following Saturday rather than wait the extra week.

'The trip's being paid for by the World Sporting Club,' he told me. 'They've been fantastic. They had a club dinner during the week and held a collection for Lillian. They raised £2,000 in about ten minutes. 'We'll spend part of that when we come out. But what shall we do with the rest? Is there anything Lillian wants?'

'What about hiring a car?' I asked. 'Lillian's very fond of going for drives and with our own car we can please ourselves how far we go and when we go.'

'Right,' George said. 'I'll ask Jack Solomons (the boxing promoter). He's holding the money for us.'

During the next few weeks Lillian continued her remarkable improvement. She had no pain, ate well and was anxious to get out and about. We went on a couple of shopping expeditions to Rottach-Egern to find her some warmer winter clothes and bought snow boots, thick ski-pants and sweaters. The removal of her tonsils ended the outings temporarily, however, as she was confined to her room for three days as a safeguard against infection. Again Lillian went through the minor operation without a murmur, even though it was carried out only with pain killing injections. Dr Issels was against anaesthetic because of its weakening effect.

The doctors were amazed by Lillian's recovery from the tonsillectomy. Within two hours she was feeling hungry, after three they asked her not to talk so much in case she reopened the incision and after five they were having to reason with her to stop her taking an afternoon walk through the clinic's grounds. By the following morning her throat was almost completely healed. 'I have never seen anything like it before,' one of the dentists said. 'Always people are in bed for two or three days. You are better after only a few hours.'

Meanwhile the letters from well-wishers from England had started to pour in. About a hundred and fifty a day. Some from friends, some from faith healers, some from religious people, some from cranks, but mostly from Lillian's legion of followers. They came not just from Great Britain and Southern Ireland but from Germany, France, Switzerland, South Africa and even the United States. The message in all of them, though, was summed up by a one-word telegram from Lillian's former boss, Patrick Foster. It said simply, 'Win'.

Suddenly Lillian's room at the clinic attracted even greater interest than before among the staff. Everybody seemed to be a stamp collector and each day Lillian and I would carefully sort out the stamps and leave them in bundles for the nurses and doctors. Along with the letters there also came the Press, from all parts of the continent. Lillian, as improved as she was, still was not strong enough to go through lengthy interviews and elected me as her spokesman. It was a job I didn't mind, partly because as a journalist myself I knew the reporters did not relish assignments such as this, and partly because I felt it only fair to keep the public informed in view of their tremendous response.

In the evenings I would discuss with Lillian the kind of questions I had been asked. 'Most of them seem to be going on the theme that this is your greatest race,' I told her.

'I suppose they were bound to use that,' Lillian said. 'But really this is a world away from athletics, isn't it? I'm not running in some glorious race. I've got cancer. I'm fighting to live. Athletics don't even come into it. What good are medals and records to me now?'

I realised then that Lillian hadn't been taken in by my explanation that she had 'a mild form of cancer' for long. Her chats with other patients had gradually told her that she was seriously ill. But she had taken it in her stride and, as her knowledge grew, so did her determination to fight.

The thing that impressed us as much as any about the clinic was the open relationship between doctor and patient. Most patients knew the precise state of their condition and could follow their day-to-day progress on a comprehensive chart hung just over their bed. Information was kept from them only in extreme cases and even then relatives were told exactly what was happening. In fact, the participation of relatives and friends in helping patients was encouraged strongly. The doctors preferred them to stay by the bedside during all kinds of treatment and once I was even handed a white overall and asked to help.

Lillian quickly struck up friendships with the nurses, who were far more friendly and helpful than any she had met before. The house sister, Frauke, even lent her her own record player and records when Lillian happened to mention how much she loved music.

The car the World Sporting Club had hired for us turned out to be an automatic Mercedes. It was delivered on the

Saturday morning, in time for me to meet Lillian's parents at Munich Airport. It was the first time I had driven an automatic and the first time I had driven on the right. That, coupled with the fact that after I had met everybody I had a full car and couldn't see out of the back window, and was unsure of the route anyway, gave us a couple of anxious moments as we circled the city three times trying to find the road to Rottach-Egern. But nobody seemed to mind very much. They were all elated at the thought of seeing Lillian again.

The weekend went well. Lillian, bored at being cooped up in her room because of her tonsils, was both delighted and stimulated by everybody's arrival. Her parents were as impressed with the clinic and Dr Issels as I had been and it was with a great feeling of hope that they travelled back to England the following Monday. It had been decided that Irene would take a fortnight off work and stay in Bavaria when her parents went home. She sat with Lillian while I ran George, Frances and my mother to the airport.

'Those weeks in St Mark's seem to belong to a different world,' George said as we drove along, echoing the thoughts I had had a few days earlier. 'I'll be able to sleep well tonight for the first time in what feels like years. I'm sure we did the right thing bringing Lillian here. We can never have any regrets about that.'

When I arrived back at the clinic I stopped by the main house to collect the post. The Austrian woman from Haus Lipp was sitting in a corner of the reception hall. She was obviously upset and I decided it was best to leave her alone. But as I stood waiting for the letters to be handed to me I heard someone speaking to her.

'How is your brother-in-law?' they asked.

'He's dead,' she said with a sob, '. . . a few minutes ago.'

Selfishly, I got out of the building as quickly as possible. Death, as far as I was concerned, was a thing which just didn't happen at the clinic. I didn't want to hear anything which would tear open the cosy cocoon I had wrapped myself in. Subconsciously, though, that incident coloured my future relationships with relatives of patients. Unless I was sure the news would be good, I never again asked for condition reports and, to a degree, I tried to keep out of their way. I knew it was anti-social but there was worry enough over Lillian without forming friendships which would possibly end in grief. The only important thing was that Lillian should be as happy as possible and sheltered from the harsher realities.

During the next few weeks others died, but by then I was conditioned to accept it. My initial sadness gave way to a cold-blooded appraisal of the odds. I sheltered in the logic that if Dr Issels claimed a seventeen per cent success rate, then of the present patients about a hundred would die to put Lillian in the survival area. And, terrible as it seems looking back, I found myself half-prepared to write off everybody else provided Lillian came out all right.

Lillian revelled in Irene's company during the early days of her stay—before Dr Issels discovered a new problem which was to hinder his therapy throughout.

'Our X-rays show Lillian still has large quantities of barium inside her stomach,' he said. 'And the whole of her stomach below the colotomy is impacted.'

It seemed unbelievable. Barium still in Lillian's stomach more than three months after she had first taken it?

'I do not understand why she was left in such a condition,' said Dr Issels angrily. 'It means she has poison running throughout her body . . . and that must be cleared if my therapy is to succeed.'

It was the start of a series of complicated enemas which Lillian underwent almost daily during the last few weeks of her life. Slowly the blockage cleared, but it also meant the end of pain-free days. Her morale dropped, her appetite diminished and she was forced to go back on injections which eased her discomfort but weakened her body.

She was still determined to get out whenever possible, though, and after we had been at the clinic thirteen days she asked for, and received, permission to have lunch in one of Tegernsee's most expensive hotels, 'The Bachmair'. We had strict instructions on what she was allowed to eat and, as meat was still banned, Lillian settled for trout. I watched her with admiration as she ate her meal. Despite everything, she still carried herself with grace and dignity. She had that indefinable thing called style—and nothing could take that away.

Dr Issels' sixty-fourth birthday was one of the major topics of conversation among the nurses at the clinic at that time, for he always put on a lavish party. Lillian insisted on going out to choose a card for him, but the awaited day, November 21st, brought a crisis instead of a celebration. She started to feel very ill that afternoon as she sat with Irene and me in a small cafe about a quarter of a mile from the clinic. She was drinking a cup of herbal tea when suddenly she had acute pains in her stomach and felt sick.

We returned to the clinic immediately, called the nurses and put Lillian to bed. Her condition did not improve and eventually Dr Issels was called from his birthday party. He looked grave as he examined Lillian and then motioned for Irene and me to talk to him outside. Lillian was busy with one of the nurses, so we slipped out quietly.

'The tumour in her stomach has swollen,' Dr Issels said. 'If it does not go down her condition is very critical. Her parents should be told.'

I looked at Irene and the expression on her face told me she was feeling the same as me. 'I know it sounds bad,' I told her. 'But I'm sure it will be O.K. I've just got that sort of feeling.'

'Yes, I know,' she said. 'I should be worried, but I'm not. I'm sure Lillian will be all right.'

I did telephone George and Frances, but told them merely that Lillian wasn't feeling so well that day and that she was looking forward to seeing them soon . . . perhaps they could come out again in a few days?

Dr Issels wanted me to stay with Lillian that night in case of emergencies, so the nurses equipped me with blankets and pillows and I camped down on the floor of her room. She was given several injections which I was told should reduce the tumour and, in fact, by midnight was feeling a little better.

I stayed awake until the early hours, and my conviction

that Lillian would recover strengthened as I saw she was sleeping soundly. By morning the pains had gone and together we searched for a reason for her sudden relapse. We remembered that she had had a packet of crisps the previous afternoon as a 'treat'. It had been a break from the strict diet, but had seemed harmless enough. I desperately wanted to find a reason to stop Lillian from worrying and that seemed as good as any. 'Yes, it must have been that,' Lillian agreed. 'From now on I'll eat only what I'm told I can.'

I called George and Frances again that evening, told them the relapse was over and outlined the full seriousness of the incident. But I needn't have bothered. George had already read something into my tone the previous night and he and Frances had made arrangements to fly out the following Tuesday, November 24th.

'A fund has been started over here by Marea Hartman,' George told me. 'They've collected thousands. It's overwhelming to think how well loved Lillian must be. Some of the money has been sent to help us come out and visit Lillian. So we were already thinking of coming out soon . . . before your call made us realise something was wrong.'

Lillian was delighted to be seeing her parents again so soon and also about the news of the fund; not so much from the money aspect as knowing that people genuinely cared about her—whether or not she was winning races.

Dr Issels waited until Lillian's parents had arrived before telling us he wanted Lillian to have a small operation at the nearby Tegernsee Hospital. 'It will be like a second colotomy,' he said. 'But it is vital if we are to clear the poison from her stomach.'

We telephoned the hospital the afternoon after the operation and were told it had gone well. Lillian was being kept in the intensive care unit just as a precaution and we could visit her any time.

The first person we saw when we arrived was the anaesthetist. 'Everything all right?' we asked eagerly, confident he would reiterate what we had been told on the telephone. Instead, he looked grave. 'It is a very sad case,' he said. 'We can do no more to help.'

I felt the shock ripple between us. 'Why? What do you mean? The operation was all right, wasn't it?'

'Yes,' he said, but with an air of uncertainty. 'Anyway, you can see her for yourself.'

We hurried to the intensive care unit and stood there almost too scared to open the door. The anaesthetist led the way and as we stepped into the ward I could feel the relief wave over me, leaving me exhausted.

Lillian looked up from her bed with a cheerful wave. 'It was nothing like my first colotomy,' she said. 'I've got hardly any pain. When do I go back to the clinic?'

The anaesthetist was still looking serious when we went back outside. 'A very sad case,' he said.

Suddenly we realised he was talking about Lillian's general condition. And whereas we had learnt to live with the fact and look beyond that in a bid to get her better, for strangers it was still, obviously, the essential factor when we asked after her condition. For the first time I understood fully what a complete brainwashing job I had done on myself in those early weeks in Bavaria.

Lillian stayed in hospital for four days during which time Marea Hartman arrived from England and Irene returned home. With the backing of the fund money behind them, George and Frances decided they would remain in Bavaria for as long as necessary, much to Lillian's delight.

The day before Lillian returned from Tegernsee I was summoned to Dr Issels' office. I knew that it must be something urgent for him to seek me out, a fear substantiated by what he had to tell me.

'I was present during Lillian's operation in Tegernsee,' he said. 'I'm sorry to have to tell you that her stomach is filled by a mass of tumour. I fear that my therapy is too small to fight all of it. I think she has come here too late. But, of course, we say nothing of this to Lillian, and I will not tell her parents yet. I may still be able to help and I do not want them to worry more than they are.'

I felt the same sort of depression that had weighed so heavily in London as I left, but a sudden development two days later brought back all the hope, and doubly so. Dr

Issels was just finishing a routine examination on Lillian that afternoon when he turned to me with a look of delight. 'The rectum tumour has gone down by a third,' he said.

I was still feeling elated when the telephone rang outside Lillian's room later that night. It was the *Daily Express*. Another progress check, I thought, and was working out what to tell them when I realised the voice on the other end was talking about something different. 'Lillian has been voted Sportswoman of the Year,' it said. 'Could you tell her and ask her how she feels about it?'

Lillian was a little stunned at first, and then bubbled over with joy. 'Why, it's not even as if I've been competing at all well this season,' she said amazed. 'Tell them it's wonderful, but I feel a little guilty about having done nothing to really deserve it.'

'You've done everything to deserve it,' I told her. 'You've inspired millions over these past few weeks. And at least now you've got the final bit of proof that people are fond of you as much as a person as an athlete.'

The news delighted everybody at the clinic and, as if by way of celebration, Dr Issels made a point of speaking to me the following day.

'It all goes well,' he said. 'Better than I thought possible. If we can continue like this for a fortnight I am really hopeful.'

14

THE LAST CHAPTER

The turning point came on Friday, December 11th. I arrived at House Diana at eight-thirty a.m. and the look on the nurses' faces told me immediately that something was wrong.

'Lillian is not so well,' one of them said as I walked in through the door. 'Dr Freda is with her.' There had been scares before, but something in her tone made me feel that this was the most serious of them all. I raced up the stairs and opened the door to Lillian's room. Dr Freda looked round as I went in and I could see the worry etched across her face. Lillian was being carried out of bed by two of the nurses.

'They're moving me to the main house,' she said. 'I had a bad night.'

'She will be better there,' Dr Freda said quickly . . . a bit too quickly. 'There will be people to look after her twenty-four hours a day. I had to come to her seven times during the night to give injections.'

'It's the intensive care unit,' Lillian told me, but I already knew. And people could call it what they liked but to me it was the death house. Nobody, as far as I knew, died in out-lying wards such as House Diana. But they did in House One.

Suddenly I was frightened. Ever since we had arrived at the clinic I had dreaded Lillian being moved to House One. To me it was just one step away from death and I felt that as long as she was in House Diana she was safe. Frances and

George walked in just as Lillian was being helped on with her dressing gown and the look on their faces when they heard the news told me they felt the same. Heidi, the ward sister, must have sensed it, too. 'She can come back here as soon as she has recovered from last night,' she said reassuringly. But words were past helping.

George and I carried Lillian downstairs to the car and drove the two hundred yards to the big white chateau. George went back to help Frances collect Lillian's things while a male nurse and I carried Lillian to the first floor ward.

It was the first time I had been upstairs in the main house. I had called at the reception hall dozens of times to collect mail and make phone calls, but I had always felt the need to hurry out. Its sparse, business-like furniture and the huge statue of Christ which overhung the main staircase brought home so forcefully the reason we were there. Over in House Diana I could lose myself in the unreality of picture postcard views and guest house style rooms.

A long corridor ran the length of the first floor in House One. There were no carpets, no ornaments; nothing that gave a pretence of welcome. Lillian's room was in stark contrast to the one she had just left: a washbasin, a plain wardrobe and a heavy metal hospital-style bed. There was no illusion of glamour here. Even the nurses, handpicked for their attractiveness in the other wards, were highly competent, but ordinary. This was the nerve centre of Issels' clinic, a grim arena of life and death struggles that had no place for the squeamish or the sensitive. As I looked around Lillian's room the past four weeks vanished as if a dream. Cancer isn't pretty views or attractive nurses, I told myself. It's this. A stark, functional room in a stark, functional building. Lillian, though, seemed fairly happy about the move. It was as if being back in familiar hospital surroundings made her feel something more comprehensible was being done to get her better.

Lillian's new house doctor was Dr Christian Lentrodt, a tall intense man of about thirty-five, said to be Issels' brightest protégé. He was handsome in a lean, angular way with a flashing smile and a good command of Americanised English. 'Lillian was in pain last night because the tumour has swollen again,' he said. 'We will reduce it.' After a series of injections, the tumour did shrink a little during the afternoon, but Lillian still needed several pain-killing injections. She recovered in the evening, though, to eat a good meal and I left her that night thinking the worst was over.

Meanwhile Irene, her fiancé Frank Hayes, Lillian's brother George and my mother had arrived in Rottach-Egern ready for what had been planned as a reunion on Lillian and Irene's twenty-second birthday on Sunday, the 13th. Marea Hartman was arriving the next morning. I had had a few misgivings ever since the 'party' had been planned. It had seemed to be tempting Providence, although, of course, Lillian wanted to see her family on her birthday.

I met everybody back at the hotel in which George and Frances were staying and told them Lillian had settled comfortably for the night. We decided I would go to the clinic on my own as usual in the morning and if Lillian was all right the others could follow on in twos or threes so as not to overcrowd her.

After the relaxed mood in which I had left her I was confident of finding Lillian much better in the morning. So when I opened the door to her room at eight a.m., the sight that confronted me came as a double shock and I could feel my nerve crack as certainly as if I had crushed a twig. Lillian was hunched in a drugged stupor in the centre of the bed, every limb in her body trembling. She tried to lift her head at the sound of the door but failed. She was moaning quietly to herself and as I drew nearer I could hear her saying, 'Injection . . . injection.'

I wanted to call a nurse, run out of the room and then come back in a few hours' time to be told it had all been my imagination. Instead, I called the nurse and made myself wait there as calmly as possible until she arrived. She was a rather severe-looking girl, hardened beyond her years by the sights she had seen. 'Lillian has had too many injections,' she said. 'That is why she is so weak. She is asking for them now out of habit. She does not really need one . . . and she must have no more for some time.'

I sat there for a couple of hours, talking Lillian into sleeping on and off. Gradually the trembling lessened and she began to speak to me in something like her usual voice. George and Frances arrived to find her very weak and in a little pain. It was obvious there was no chance of everybody seeing her that day.

Dr Issels visited Lillian mid-way through the morning with Dr Lentrodt. There was none of the usual joking banter and they looked more serious than I had ever seen them when they finished the examination. They conversed in hurried German and a sharp order sent a nurse hurrying for some apparatus. 'There is much fluid in Lillian's abdomen,' Dr Issels said. 'We must try to drain some away.' They worked solidly at the minor operation for an hour and by the time they had finished they had drawn off three and a half litres of water. Dr Issels left still looking grave. 'Someone must be here tonight,' he said. 'All the time.'

We arranged that George and Frances would stay for the afternoon and evening and I would take over for the night. But at ten p.m. as I got ready to return to the clinic I suddenly realised I was terrified.

'For the first time I'm really scared,' I said to my mother. 'Just to sit there waiting for something awful to happen. I don't know if I can do it any more, I feel as if my nerves have been shattered.'

'I'll come with you,' she said, and together we drove apprehensively back to the clinic.

Lillian had relapsed into her early morning condition and my fears were heightened when I saw that the nurses were looking into her room every ten minutes to check her pulse. 'This is really serious,' I said to my mother. 'They've never done all this before. They must think she's going to die tonight.' I tried to talk myself into believing it would turn out all right. 'It's the 13th tomorrow,' I argued. 'My lucky day . . . and Lillian's birthday. Nothing can happen tonight, surely?'

At midnight George suddenly arrived at the clinic. He

looked tired after his long vigil that afternoon, but he insisted on staying with me and sending my mother back to the hotel. Lillian was sleeping by this time, so we settled down in the nearby nurses' room where we could watch the alarm lights from the various rooms. These flickered on and off incessantly and every time there was one from Lillian's section of the building we raced into the corridor to see if it was hers.

Meanwhile, the nurses continued their constant check on Lillian's condition. After each time they nodded to show all was still well, but at two-thirty their mood suddenly seemed to change. George was sitting in a corner of the room dozing a little and did not seem to notice. I did not disturb him, but tackled the nurse the next time she went out of the room.

'What's wrong?' I asked. 'Something has happened, hasn't it?'

She seemed reluctant to speak for several seconds but then said, 'Let's say she is sleeping very deeply.'

'You mean a coma?'

She nodded almost imperceptibly.

'But she'll be O.K., won't she?'

'I cannot say. I have telephoned the doctor and he has told me to give her a heart injection. I cannot give her another for two hours. We must wait.'

I walked down the stairs to the front door to have a much needed breath of air and as I looked out at the sky I saw the moon was surrounded by a perfect circle of brilliant light. It was a phenomenon I had never seen before and I felt an eerie, crawling sensation down my back. But at the same time I was strangely uplifted. If it's a sign I wanted, I told myself, surely this is it? Lillian's going to pull through.

I returned to join George in the duty room and sat there counting off the minutes until daylight. I was just starting to relax a little when Lillian's emergency light flashed on at five a.m. The nurse leapt from her seat and hurried into the corridor. I followed her out and as she opened Lillian's door I could see Lillian standing unsteadily on her feet near the washbasin. 'Oh, hello,' she said. 'I was trying to have a wash and thought I'd need a bit of help.'

I went out of the room quicker than I had gone in, so Lillian wouldn't see my tears of relief. 'Now she must be all right,' I told myself over and over. 'She's come through this. It must mean she's destined to get better.'

Lillian's brother, George, and Frank arrived soon afterwards and I left the clinic at about seven-thirty a.m. On the way out I saw Dr Issels' car pull into the driveway. He stopped and got out. 'The nurse has told me all is well,' he said. 'I have not slept at all last night. I thought she would die. But now we have the chance again.'

Lillian continued on the critical list throughout the day, but by the evening she had recovered a little. George and I maintained our vigil in the duty room that night, but it passed quietly with Lillian sleeping well. Her strength returned throughout the following morning and by the afternoon she was enough her old self to bring up the question of marriage.

'I know I wouldn't be able to do a lot around the house for some time,' she told me with a look of apology that cut me in half. 'But do you think we'll be able to get married when I get back from here?'

'Of course we will,' I told her. 'We can always get someone in to do the housework. That's the last thing you want to worry about. I'll take a long holiday and we can do all the things you've missed over the past few months. I promise you, I'll make up for all you've suffered.'

I called back at the clinic at midnight but the nurses told me Lillian was sleeping peacefully and there was no danger. The crisis, it seemed had passed. The legacy, though, left Lillian very weak and Dr Issels made it our responsibility to see Lillian eat a little and often. 'She must eat eight times a day,' he said. 'Always a little and always very good chew, chew. The tumour is going down, but she must get back her strength.' And slowly, but surely she did. We asked, reasoned, pleaded and threatened until each day she had eaten her quota of food and drunk her quota of liquid and each day her weight went up and the swelling of her stomach went down. The pain disappeared, Lillian's frame of mind grew happier and Dr Issels lost his worried look each time he started to examine her. 'It all goes well,' he told us. And it did. So much so that we had ideas of Lillian being moved back to House Diana.

Then, on Monday, December 21st, everything collapsed. That afternoon Dr Issels decided it would ease Lillian's discomfort even further if some more water was drained from her stomach where it had been collecting each day. But within half an hour of starting the operation he came out of Lillian's room shaking his head and looking dreadfully worried. He called together a couple more of the doctors and went back inside.

Frances was beside herself with anxiety as we sat waiting in the corridor. I was finding it hard to keep calm myself, so eventually I opened Lillian's door and slipped into her room. The faces all around Lillian's bed were tense. Using the little German I had picked up over the weeks I realised they were discussing the colour of the fluid they were drawing off. I looked at one of the jugs. The contents were a muddy brown colour, far different from the almost clear water they had drawn off the previous time. After a few minutes Dr Issels beckoned to me to come outside. 'Please come down to my office,' he said. 'And bring the parents and sister with you.' We seated ourselves around his desk, staring into his grave expression, fearing what he was about to say.

'I'm sorry to tell you Lillian has peritonitis,' he said. 'It is a thing I have always been afraid of. It means she is lost. I can do no more.'

'What is peritonitis?' I asked.

'It means she has a puncture of the abdomen and that she will grow weaker and weaker until she dies.'

And I found myself again asking that awful question, 'How long?'

'Two or three days. But, of course, we say nothing to Lillian. We will let her eat anything she wants, anything at all. And she can stay here. But I can do no more to help.'

We sat there in a seemingly everlasting silence. Surely he could offer us just one more grain of hope? I looked at Frances and Irene and I could sense that, like me, they did not really believe this was happening. How could we have come this far and been through so much to have it end like this?

Dr Issels started talking again. 'There is the question of an autopsy. It is entirely up to you, of course. But I know what I would do if she were my daughter. It would tell us just how she died, how long the cancer had been growing. And it would probably help other patients in the future.' The request went completely over my head. I still was not convinced about peritonitis, let alone ready to start thinking about autopsies. But George was saying, 'We want to thank you, doctor, for all you've done. No one could have done more. If an autopsy will help others then perhaps it would be a good thing.'

I rose to leave, to get back up and see Lillian and reassure myself that she was still feeling no pain. Until she showed another marked decline I wasn't even going to consider the thought that she only had a few days to live.

Lillian smiled cheerfully as I went in. 'I'm glad that's over,' she said. 'But I do feel hungry. Do you think they've got any liver sausage and tomatoes in the kitchen?' The relief spread through me. We're not finished yet, I told myself, and hurried down to the kitchen. But it was deserted, the staff had gone home and the cupboards were locked.

'Don't worry,' I told Lillian. 'I'll go back to the hotel and get you some from there. I'll only be a few minutes.'

I was back inside half an hour and ran up the stairs to her room holding a huge parcel of salad the hotel had rustled up. But as I turned into the corridor I saw Lillian being wheeled away into the lift. I felt a moment's panic. Surely they weren't moving her out to fly her home? Hadn't Issels said she could stay?

Lillian saw me just in time. 'I'm going to Munich,' she called. 'Apparently I've got peritonitis and I've got to have a small operation to put it right.'

With my mind reeling I charged into Dr Issels' office. 'Ah, David,' he said. 'I've just telephoned Dr Rudolph Zenker in Munich. He is the best surgeon in Germany and he thinks he can operate to save Lillian. But she must go immediately. An ambulance is already on its way.'

'We're going too,' I said, and stormed out of the door after George and Frances who had gone back with Irene to her lodgings in a nearby guest house.

Snow had been falling all day and as I ran in an insane, joyful excitement, I crashed over time and again. Hadn't I told myself it would all be all right? One moment all is lost, the next Lillian's off to Munich for an operation that will save her. It's just fate. That's it . . . fate. She's just destined to get better. I pounded on Irene's door and barged inside dripping with snow and sweat. 'We're off to Munich . . . an operation . . . Lillian can be saved . . .' I said in a mad rush. 'We must hurry, she's waiting to go.'

Our hire car had been due to be fitted with snow tyres the following day, but there was no time to worry about that. 'I don't care if we crash thirty times over,' said Irene. 'Just as long as we get there.' The snow started to fall heavily as we set off in the wake of the ambulance and by the time we reached the Autobahn it was whipping down in the strongest blizzard I had seen. A dozen times I lost the back wheels as we sped along roads covered at least three inches thick. But only once did we come close to an accident, when the rear wing bumped against a rocky wall as we went broadside down a steep, winding hill. We had taken an English-speaking nurse with us as navigator, which was just as well, for we soon lost the snow-equipped ambulance. Even so, we covered the fifty kilometres to Munich in just over an hour and found our way to Dr Zenker's Chirurgische Klinik der Universität.

Lillian was already settled in her new bed and had been examined by a doctor when we found her room. 'They say now it might not be peritonitis,' she told us. 'Anyway, they're not operating tonight. They've decided to make a final decision tomorrow.'

Dr Zenker's second-in-command confirmed what Lillian had told us, so we left her to rest while we found a hotel. After a couple of fruitless enquiries we eventually booked in at the Ambassador Hotel, only about half a mile away from the Chirurgische Klinik. The receptionist looked me up and down as I made the registration. 'This is an expensive hotel,' he said. 'Are you sure you can afford it?' For the first time I realised that I must look a bit of a mess. I had buttoned up my coat wrongly in the rush, my cravat was half way round the back of my neck and my hair was still matted with drying snow. Also none of us had any luggage. Luckily, though, George had had the presence of mind to grab some travellers' cheques and a handful of German marks from our kitty and he quickly waved these in front of the receptionist's face. 'We'll pay in advance, if you like,' he said. But the point had already been made.

We returned to the clinic early the next morning to find Lillian in fine form. The doctors told us there was no peritonitis and that Lillian would probably be returning to Rottach-Egern the following day. Dr Issels called on us in Munich that afternoon and explained how the mistake had occurred. It seemed that because of the cancer one of Lillian's intestines was stuck to her stomach wall. The probe Dr Issels had inserted to drain off the fluid had pierced the intestine. He had thought the fluid he was draining off had come from outside her stomach when in fact it was coming from the inside. 'It was a million to one chance,' he said. 'Never have I heard anything like it before.'

We began to make plans for a return to Rottach-Egern. We were all eager for Lillian to get back and resume the treatment. Also we hoped to spend Christmas among friends rather than in the bleak surroundings of an almost-deserted Munich. But just as we were making the final arrangements Dr Zenker informed us he had decided to operate after all. There was a small blockage in the stomach, he said, and while Lillian was in a surgical hospital it might just as well be cleared. Dr Issels had been told and was in agreement.

The operation was done on the Wednesday afternoon. Lillian did her usual job of reassuring us. 'Don't worry, Daddy!' she called to George as she waited for the lift to take her to the theatre. 'I'll be all right. I just wish they'd hurry up—I'm hungry.' They were to be the last clear words she spoke to her father. Dr Issels called to see her that evening. 'You've a very brave girl,' he told her. 'But this will be the last operation. How would you say it in sport? The last hurdle? Now we can get to work to get you better.' Lillian gave him a broad smile and the thumbs-up. 'The last hurdle,' she said. 'Marvellous.'

By mid-day Thursday Lillian had recovered from the after-effects of the operation except that she was unable to eat solid food and had to be fed intravenously. The drips were going constantly, some for food, some for blood plasma, some for vitamins. And every couple of hours one of the nuns, who comprised the majority of the nurses, would administer a series of injections. Lillian took it all without a murmur even though she had to lie still for hours so as not to dislodge the various tubes.

Glancing through the various Munich papers in our hotel that night I noticed several of them had given a lot of space to Lillian's arrival in the city. As I read what I could understand of the various stories my admiration grew for Dr Issels. For I discovered that Dr Zenker had been one of the prime movers in bringing the manslaughter charge against him in 1961. In our hour of desperate need, Issels had sacrificed his pride to ask Zenker for help.

As in Rottach-Egern, Frances, George, Irene and I split the day into shifts so that someone was with Lillian all the time. Irene and I were with Lillian during Thursday afternoon. Lillian was dozing off and on, but each time she woke she was more talkative than for a long time. She started to play at make-believe. 'It's Christmas Eve tomorrow,' she said. 'Shall we have a party? Who shall we invite?'

Irene entered into the spirit of it. 'Well, we can all come. And perhaps Dr Issels and some of the nurses will come down for the evening.'

'What shall we eat?' I asked Lillian.

'Oh, all the things I haven't been allowed to have over the past few weeks . . . cream cakes, chocolates, perhaps even a gin and tonic. I've always looked forward to spending Christmas with you. We must make the most of it.'

As we elaborated on the idea, Lillian's speech gradually

became more slurred. I thought at first she was just tired. But then I saw her eyes were glazed and slightly staring. I walked anxiously across to the bed and put my hand on her arm.

'Are you all right?'

She gripped my hand tightly. 'You don't think I'm funny, do you,' she asked in a strange voice. 'Please say you don't.'

'Of course not,' I said, getting really worried. I tried to take my hand away so I could go and find a nurse, but she gripped it even tighter. Slowly I drew it free and walked quickly to the nurses' room.

'Lillian has gone a little dizzy,' I told one of the nuns. 'I think it must be some of the drugs.'

The nun hurried into Lillian's room and disconnected one of the drips. 'Ah, yes,' she said. 'This drug does affect some people. I will give her another to counteract it.'

But over the next half hour Lillian lapsed slowly into unconsciousness. We grew more and more worried and I could see the nuns, too, were beginning to think it unusual. They stepped up the speed of the new drip and this seemed to help a little. Lillian regained consciousness, recognised us and even managed to talk a little. The danger seemed over and when George and Frances arrived to allow us to get something to eat there seemed little point in mentioning the incident and worrying them unnecessarily.

We returned a few hours later to find Lillian much the same as we had left her. But as the evening wore on her condition deteriorated again. The doctors, at first puzzled, began to look increasingly anxious as she drifted deeper and deeper into a semi-coma. Her breathing became laboured and we could get no response when we called her name. Suddenly the senior doctor rapped a quick command and a nurse disappeared to return with an oxygen machine. 'You must call her parents,' he said to me. 'They must come . . . now.'

I telephoned George and Frances at the hotel, trying to keep the panic out of my voice as much as possible as I sketched out a little of what was happening. They arrived within a few minutes and one look at the commotion inside Lillian's room told them all I hadn't said. Together we moved back into the well of the corridor where the staff had erected a giant Christmas tree, complete with glass balls and tinsel. Behind it, in front of large stained-glass windows which looked out into the street stood a miniature Nativity crib.

The senior doctor joined us a few moments later. 'We are not certain what is wrong,' he said. 'But we think it could be a blood clot on the brain . . . caused by the cancer. We have arranged for one of Munich's top neurologists to call later to see her.' The neurologist, a woman, came after an hour. She confirmed the doctor's fears.

'This obviously means she is seriously ill,' the doctor told us. 'But we will do all we can. There is no immediate danger. By that I mean I do not think she will die tonight.'

Irene and I said we would stay with Lillian that night and the hospital arranged for a nurse to be at her bedside throughout. As we sat there that night listening to distant carol singers in one of the side streets, I felt for the first time since we arrived in Germany that Lillian would not re-cover. I was empty, devoid of almost all hope. There was a limit to what even inspired medicine could achieve and it looked as if we had reached it. The times I'd wished I could see into the future during those past months. And to think it would probably end in an orthodox German hospital, hardly different from the ones Lillian had been in back home, with cold snow all around us in an empty city, closed for the week as people prepared to celebrate Christmas. Lillian spent a quiet night, hardly moving. Her breathing grew laboured around three a.m. but by day-break had settled into a steady rhythm.

George and Frances arrived early that morning and Irene and I went back to the hotel to rest. But I found it impossible to sleep. The past weeks had finally caught up and I felt dreadful. I lay wide-eyed in bed, my stomach churning as I waited for the harsh snarl of the door bell or the gentle trill of the bedside phone which could only bring news I didn't want to hear. At mid-day the phone rang. It was Frances.

'David,' she said. 'You'd better get round here as fast as possible.' I called Irene and we ran round to the clinic. But as we ran something told me that Lillian would still be all right when we got there. As much as I felt that Lillian's fight was nearly over, I was sure it had not ended yet.

Lillian's room was crowded with nurses and doctors and the oxygen machine was again working furiously. One of the younger doctors asked to speak to George and me. 'We have reached the stage where it is difficult to know what to do,' he said. 'We can stop all treatment, in which case she will die quickly, or we can try to do everything. It will be extremely expensive and can have almost no chance of success.'

We had come too far now to even consider letting any chance pass, no matter how non-existent.

'Try everything,' said George. 'Everything.'

The oxygen and a series of injections again calmed Lillian and for one split second it seemed one of the nurses had broken through her coma when Lillian moved a little as her name was called. But she was only shifting her position in her sleep.

George and I stayed in her room that night, but there were no further emergencies. Christmas Day also passed quietly and the doctors told us it would be better for us not to stay that night, but get some sleep instead. George refused to leave, though, and again bedded down in Lillian's room. I sat with him until one a.m., then went back to the hotel. I was finding it impossible to keep still wherever I was. As soon as I reached the clinic and found Lillian was still all right, I wanted to get back to the hotel rather than sit there watching every breath she drew and praying it would not be the last. As soon as I got back to the hotel I wanted to go round to the clinic again.

Irene and I stayed with Lillian during the morning of Boxing Day. As we sat there a nurse called in to say there was a phone call from London. I took it in the duty room. A man introduced himself and said he represented a church in England. 'The doctors have done all they can,' he said. 'Only prayer can help now. I want to say one through you for Lillian. I am sure she can be saved.'

We had received so many religious pamphlets and charms through the post that our early gratitude had given way to scepticism. But the man was obviously so sincere that I agreed and tried to recapture my frame of mind of only a few days ago when I had been certain Lillian would recover. He said two short prayers and as I said 'Amen' to the second I felt again a little stirring of hope. We returned to the hotel at two-thirty when George and Frances came to take over and were sitting drinking coffee when the phone rang at two minutes past four. 'David,' said Frances, 'please call Irene and come round as quickly as possible.' Again we raced to the clinic but when we were fifty yards short of the door I said to Irene, 'Slow down a little and get your breath back. Try to relax a bit.'

Something had told me it was all over and I wanted both of us to be composed ready for the next few minutes. By an eerie coincidence a radio in a street restaurant near the clinic was playing Guantanamera as we pushed open the clinic doors. I could feel the cold sweat on my hands and an almost drunken lightheadedness as we turned into the corridor leading to Lillian's room. Frances was at the door waiting for us. Her face was a mask of disbelief and she was clenching her hands in front of her.

'It's over,' she said, and the effort of speech brought the tears. 'She's gone . . . almost as soon as I put the phone down. George was holding her hand, feeling her pulse and it suddenly stopped.'

I walked into the room with a feeling of dread, but it disappeared when I saw Lillian. She lay there looking so serene, peaceful at last after her months of ordeal. At least, I told myself, she had always been convinced she would get better. She had been spared the mental anguish and that was worth any price.

A single red candle, lit by one of the nuns, burnt brightly in the background as we gathered around the bed for our last farewell, and the smoke that wafted from it was a pyre for my future dreams. But I knew the love I had felt for Lillian during the past brief year would fill my lifetime.

⊙⊙⊙⊙⊙

TRIBUTES TO LILLIAN

WINDSOR CASTLE
  26 XII 70

MY HUSBAND AND I ARE SO MUCH DIS-
TRESSED TO HEAR OF THE DEATH OF YOUR
DAUGHTER WE SEND YOU BOTH OUR SIN-
CERE SYMPATHY

ELIZABETH R

LONDON
  26 XII 70

MY COLLEAGUES AND I SEND YOU OUR MOST
SINCERE SYMPATHY ON THE TRAGIC LOSS
AT SUCH AN EARLY AGE OF YOUR DAUGHTER
LILLIAN WHOM THE BRITISH PEOPLE LOVED
AND ADMIRED SO MUCH

EDWARD HEATH

Isles of Scilly
28 XII 70

Dear Mr and Mrs Board,

May I express to you, on behalf of my wife and myself, our deepest sympathy with you in your tragic loss. However superb the courage which your daughter showed, however unstinted the public admiration and sympathy which have been shown, none of this can for one moment derogate from your own loss and sense of suffering.

It was our privilege, now treasured more than ever, to have entertained her as our guest at No 10 on a number of occasions. She was invited to do honour, by her very presence, to distinguished overseas visitors, because she was herself so clearly an embodiment of the courage and achievement of modern Britain. And our overseas guests, to whom her name was already a legend, were flattered that she came.

I remember, too, her kindness and self-sacrifice in coming, as a superb athlete, to give encouragement to our paraplegic guests, athletes and medal-winners in a more restricted sphere—how she went to such infinite trouble to make them feel part of Britain's athletic achievement with her, and to touch and enrich their lives by so doing.

Nothing can ever help to fill her place in your family, but I want you to know that alongside the public tributes, and the thousands of private tributes you must be receiving, there are two more of us, privileged to have known her, if only briefly, and to have admired her, who will not forget, and who want to send our personal sympathy to you, and to her fiancé, and her sister at this time.

With deepest sympathy,

Yours very sincerely,

Harold Wilson

Other tributes to Lillian poured in from all parts of the world, but perhaps the most touching was the one sent by her 800 metre rival Vera Nikolic from Zagreb, Yugoslavia. In her simple English she wrote:

Goodbye Lillian,

You are gone from us for ever and a deep sorrow fills our hearts. I can't really understand this and I'll never be able to take this cruel fact. We girls, the runners of the 800 metres, have lost our greatest, best and dearest rival.

We were both born in the same year—1948. I happened to live my most important and sublime moments in athletics in your presence. My world record in 800 metres was reached in your London when running with you and against you, with your help.

In Athens, in the European Championships in 1969, you achieved your greatest triumph in Athletics. In your shadow I gained my most difficult victory. This victory was over myself and numerous moments of fear, self depression and crisis.

From now on, there is no tomorrow for you, dear Lillian. Your career has been ended by a cruel stroke of destiny. On and off the track you were my dear and wonderful friend and rival. I wish to express to you, in my name and those of all the other runners of my country, our respect and devotion. Please accept our thanks for everything you gave to athletics and to us in this short time.

Rest with God and thanks for everything, Lillian. We shall keep running and attempt to follow your bright and radiant example. I promise you I'll fight with all my heart and soul for the same ideal for which you gave everything. You'll stay with us on the track. Each of us will run for you from now on.

Goodbye, dear Lillian.

Bernard Baldwin, secretary of the Welsh A.A.A. and organiser of the yearly Nos Galan festival to commemorate the legendary runner Guto Nythbran, was one of Lillian's most genuine admirers and a good friend. In a letter to George he recalled how Lillian had been the Nos Galan mystery runner in 1969:

I have never before witnessed such scenes of emotion as when Lillian came running down the mountainside. Until this year, that is. Lillian died on Boxing Day and the Nos Galan was held a few days later. The biggest crowd I have ever seen in Mountain Ash turned out to pay homage to her . . . there was a deep reverence that night.

The male choir asked if they could offer their own special tribute. They sang 'Close thine eyes . . .' and many tear-stained faces afterwards told their own story.

The legend of Guto Nythbran has lived for more than 200 years in Welsh folk lore, and will probably live for ever. So will the legend of Lillian Board.

Marea Hartman M.B.E.: I feel Lillian was a symbol to many for her courage, modesty, integrity and youthfulness. She was probably one of the greatest fighters we have had on the track and she was not only modest in victory but never made excuses when she lost. I do not profess to understand all that has happened to such a fine girl in the last few months, and I never will. But I am glad she lived long enough to realise the love and respect so many people had for her.

Harold Abrahams C.B.E.: I am deeply sad at the news. I knew Lillian very well, and I watched her progress with admiration. There is no doubt she was absolutely outstanding. It must have taken tremendous courage to compete throughout 1969, as she did, with pains in her back. A tremendous personality, she was always modest about her achievements and always ready to help others. Athletics in Britain will be poorer for her passing.

Alf Cotton: Lillian was probably the greatest club girl London Olympiades ever had. She was an inspiration to us all. It is as though we have lost a daughter.

John Rodda (Guardian): In such a short period she contributed so much to athletics, much more than medal winning and records. Her vivacity, and personality mirrored the sport, its fun, the hard work, the failure and the success, perfectly.

Neil Allen (The Times): Just as important as her victories and records, to those who knew her, was the fresh, friendly personality of a girl who captivated both sports reporters and television audiences with her honesty and sense of humour. She was much more than a champion. She was also a very loyal, affectionate friend with a great zest for life. She will be long remembered as one who epitomised the best qualities of her generation in personality.

Terry O'Connor (Daily Mail): In the years to come many British women athletes will attain Olympian heights thanks to the inspiration of Lillian Board. She symbolised the finest virtues of a champion. During her short but glittering career on the track Lillian showed how to win and lose with grace.

THE CAREER OF LILLIAN BOARD

(by courtesy of *Athletics Weekly*)

The following list does not contain every competition of Lillian Board's career but it does include all her most significant performances.

KEY TO ABBREVIATIONS

ht	heat
i	indoors
int	intermediate
jnr	junior
LJ	long jump (the first measurement is in metres and the second in feet and inches)
LOAC	London Olympiades Athletic Club
m	metre
pb	personal best
relay races	(the first time is that of the team for the race and the second that of Lillian Board for her lap)
w	wind assisted
y	yards

1962 (aged 13)
May 12   George French Trophy: 4th jnr 100 y (12·1)
May 19   LOAC Championships: 3rd jnr 100 y (11·8
           w); 1st jnr 150 y (17·6 w)
Sept. 5   Leyton Junior Floodlit: 2nd 80 y (9·7)
Best Marks 100 y—11·8 w; 150 y—17·9 (17·6 w)

1963 (aged 14)
May 25   Middlesex Championships: 2nd jnr 100 y
           (11·3 downhill); 1st jnr LJ (4·90/16′ 1″)
June 8   Southern Championships: 3rd jnr 100 y
           (11·4); 1st jnr LJ (4·98/16′ 4¼″)
July 20   English Schools Championships: 1st jnr LJ
           (5·26/17′ 3″)
July 27   Women's A.A.A. Junior Championships: 6th
           100 y (12·3; 11·8 ht), 2nd LJ (5·33/17′ 5¾″)
Sept. 21   Southern I-C: 2nd jnr 100 y (11·5), 1st jnr LJ
           (5·40/17′ 8½″)
Best Marks 100 y—11·4 (11·3 downhill); 150 y—17·8,
           LJ—5·40/17′ 8½″

1964 (aged 15)
May 23   Middlesex Championships: 2nd int 100 y
           (11·3 downhill)
June 6   Southern Championships: 3rd int 100 y (11·8)
July 18   English Schools Championships: 5th int 100 y
           (11·8; 11·7 ht)
July 25   Women's A.A.A. Intermediate Champion-
           ships: 4th 100 y (11·6; 11·5 ht)
Sept. 5   Ilford: 220 y debut (25·5)
Sept. 19   Southern I-C: 3rd int 100 y (11·4)
Oct. 3   Alperton: 880 y debut (2:30·8)
Best Marks: 100 y—11·3, 220 y—25·5, 880 y—2:30·8, LJ
           —5·37/17′ 7½″

1965 (aged 16)
May 22   Middlesex Championships: 1st int 220 y
           (25·8), 1st int 880 y (2:26·0)

June	5	Southern Championships: 2nd int 220 y (25·6)
June	26	Hendon: 1st 880 y (2:20·5)
July	10	Oxford: 1st 100 y (11·1), 2nd 220 y straight-away (24·8; 24·7 ht)
July	17	English Schools Championships: 2nd int 150 y (16·8; 16·6 ht)
July	24	Women's A.A.A. Intermediate Championships: 2nd 220 y (25·8)
Aug.	14	Women's A.A.A. 4 × 100 m Championships: 1st LOAC 46·6
Aug.	22	Krefeld (WG): 2nd 100 m (12·3)
Aug.	28	Krefeld: 2nd 200 m (25·1)
Aug.	30	Reading: 1st LJ (5·80/19' 0¼")
Sept.	8	Leyton Junior Floodlit: 2nd int 100 y (10·9 w)
Nov.	20	Cosford Indoor: 1st 60 y (7·2), 1st 300 y (42·0)

Best Marks: 100 y—11·1 (10·9 w), 150 y—16·6, 200 m—25·1, 220 y(s)—24·7 w, 880 y—2:20·5, LJ—5·80/19' 0¼"

1966 (aged 17)

Jan.	29	Feltwell Indoor: 1st 60 y (7·3), 2nd 300 y (41·2), 1st LJ (5·70/18' 8½")
Feb.	12	Women's A.A.A. Indoor Championships: 2nd 60 y (7·1), 4th LJ (5·64/18' 6")
April	23	Southall: 1st 100 y (10·6 w), 2nd 440 y (58·1; debut)
April	27	Hayes: 1st 440 y (58·9)
May	15	Hayes: 2nd 100 y (11·1: eq. pb), 1st 440 y (57·2; pb)
May	21	Middlesex Championships: 3rd 100 y 11·5; 11·4 ht), 1st 220 y (25·6)
June	4	Southern Championships: 3rd 440 y (57·3)
June	12	Chiswick: 1st 220 y (25·0; pb)
July	1–2	Women's A.A.A. Championships: 2nd 440 y heat (55·7; pb) 4th 440 y semi (54·6; pb)
July	9	Prague: 1st 400 m (55·1)
Aug.	6	Commonwealth Games (Kingston): 1st 440 y ht (54·7)
Aug.	8	5th 440 y final (54·7)

Aug. 20	White City: 1st 400 m (54·9)
Sept. 10	Norbiton: 2nd LJ (5·83/19′ 1½″ w)
Sept. 18	France v Great Britain (Lille); 4th 400 m (55·9)
Nov. 19	Countess Howe CC: 1st (13:10)
Dec. 10	Havana: 1st 400 m (55·0)
Best Marks:	100 y—11·1 (10·6 w), 220—25·0, 440 y—54·6, LJ—5·70/18′ 8½″ i (5·83/19′ 1½″ w)

1967 (aged 18)

Feb. 11	Women's A.A.A. Indoor Championships: 3rd 60 m 2nd round (7·7 e)
May 6	Watford: 1st 220 y (24·8; pb)
May 14	Hayes: 3rd 220 y (24·7; pb)
May 20	Middlesex Championships: 1st 220 y (25·9), 1st 440 y (57·6)
May 27	Chiswick: 1st 440 y (55·7)
May 29	Aldershot: 1st 440 y (55·7)
June 3	Southern Championships: 1st 440 y (56·3)
June 10	Women's A.A.A. Relay Championships: LOAC 1st 4 × 110 y (46·9), 1st 4 × 220 y (1:37·6)
June 11	Brighton: 1st 440 y (54·4; pb)
June 14	Reading: 1st 880 y (2:08·7; pb)
June 30	Women's A.A.A. Championships: 1st 440 y ht (55·2)
July 1	1st 440 y final (55·3)
July 9	USA v Commonwealth (Los Angeles): 1st 400 m (52·8; pb)
July 17	European Cup Semi (Oslo): 1st 400 m (53·8)
July 22	Guildford: 1st 220 y (24·6; pb)
July 29	Hungary v Great Britain (Budapest): 1st 400 m (54·1)
Aug. 2	Poland v Great Britain (Szczecin): 1st 400 m (54·3)
Aug. 9	Americas v Europe (Montreal): 3rd 400 m (54·6)
Sept. 15	European Cup Final (Kiev): 1st 400 m (53·7)

Sept. 22	Great Britain v West Germany (White City): 1st 400 m (53·5)
Sept. 13	1st 4 × 200 m (1:35·9; Commonwealth rec)
Oct. 15	Mexico City: 4th 400 m ht (54·3)
Oct. 15	5th 400 m final (54·0)
Oct. 28	Havana: 1st 400 m (54·9)
Best Marks:	100 y—11·2, 220 y—24·6, 400 m—52·8, 880 y—2:08·7, LJ—5·60/18′ 4½″

1968 (aged 19)

May 4	Watford: 1st 100 y (11·0; pb), 1st 220 y (24·5; pb)
June 1	Southern: 1st 220 y (23·7; pb; 23·8 ht)
June 9	Brighton: 1st 440 y (54·8)
June 12	Reading: 1st 880 y (2:07·0; pb)
June 22	Moscow: 1st 400 m (53·5, 54·9 ht)
June 23	Moscow: 3rd 200 m semi (24·1)
June 30	Hayes: 3rd 100 m (11·8 w)
July 6	Guildford: 1st 100 y (10·9; pb), 1st 220 y (24·1)
July 13	Women's A.A.A. Relay Championships: LOAC—1st 4 × 100 m (45·5), 1st 4 × 200 m (1:37·7)
July 19	Women's A.A.A. Championships; 1st 800 m ht (2:05·7; pb)
July 20	2nd (1st UK finisher) 800 m final (2:02·0; pb)
July 27	Welsh Games: 1st 220 y (23·7 w)
July 29	Crystal Palace: 1st 200 m (23·9)
Aug. 3	Great Britain v West Germany (White City): 1st 200 m (23·5; pb)
Sept. 2	Great Britain v Poland (White City); 1st 400 m (53·0)
Sept. 14	Great Britain v Rest; 1st 220 y (23·6 w) 1st 4 × 110 y (45·0; world rec)
Oct. 4	Mexico City: 2nd 4 × 100 m (44·0; eq. UK rec)
Oct. 5	Mexico City: 2nd 200 m (23·4; pb)
Oct. 14	Olympics (Mexico City): 2nd 400 m ht (52·9)
Oct. 15	1st 400 m semi (52·5; pb)

Oct.	16	2nd 400 m final (52·1; UK rec)
Oct.	17	4th 200 m ht (23·4; eq. pb), 6th semi (23·4; eq. pb)
Oct.	19	3rd 4 × 100 m ht (43·9; UK rec)
Oct.	20	7th 4 × 100 m final (43·7; UK rec)

Best Marks: 100 y—10·9, 100 m—11·8 w, 200 m—23·4, 400 m—52·1, 800 m—2:02·0

1969 (aged 20)

May	24	Middlesex Championships: 1st 800 m (2:07·9)
May	31	Chiswick: 1st 200 m (23·9; 24·0 ht)
June	7	Southern Championships: 1st 400 m (53·8)
June	11	Reading: 1st 800 m (2:04·8)
June	14	Leicester: 1st 400 m (54·3)
June	22	Crystal Palace: 1st 200 m (23·8), 1st 4 × 400 m (3:37·6; world rec—52·9)
June	29	Hayes: 2nd 100 m (11·9; pb)
Aug.	3	Crystal Palace: 1st 300 m (37·9)
Aug.	12	Great Britain v USA (White City): 1st 4 × 400 m (3:36·5; Commonwealth rec—52·5)
Aug.	13	2nd 400 m (53·7)
Aug.	16	Great Britain v France (Middlesbrough): 1st 400 m (53·7), 1st 4 × 400 m (3:38·0, 53·8)
Aug.	23	Crystal Palace: 1st 400 m (53·9)
Aug.	30	Crystal Palace: 1st 800 m (2:05·1)
Sept.	1	Reading: 1st 100 y (11·2), 1st 200 m (24·7)
Sept.	16	European Championships (Athens): 1st 800 m ht (2:04·2)
Sept.	18	1st 800 m final (2:01·4; pb)
Sept.	19	2nd 4 × 400 m ht (3:34·3; Commonwealth rec—52·6)
Sept.	20	1st 4 × 400 m final (3:30·8; world rec—52·4)

Best Marks: 100 m—11·9, 200 m—23·8, 400 m—53·7, 800 m—2:01·4

1970 (aged 21)

| May | 2 | Watford: 1st 200 m (24·8), 1st 400 m (57·5) |
| May | 10 | West London: 3rd mile (4:55·7—debut) |

May 16	Rome: 2nd mile (4:44·6; pb—4:26·5 at 1500 m)
May 23	Ewell: 1st 100 m (12·5), 1st 200 m (24·8)
May 30	Southern Championships: 2nd 400 m (53·6) (55·2 ht)
June 6	Chiswick: 4th 200 m (24·2 w)
June 13	Edinburgh: 1st 4 × 800 m (8:27·0; world rec —2:07·0)
June 19	Women's A.A.A. Championships: 1st 800 m ht (2:06·8)
June 20	3rd 800 m final (2nd UK finisher) (2:05·1)
Best Marks:	100 m—12·5, 200 m—24·8 (24·2 w), 400 m—53·6, 800 m—2:05·1, 1500 m—4:26·5, mile—4:44·6

CAREER SUMMARY

Best Marks: 100 y—10·9 (10·6 w), 100 m—11·9 (11·8 w), 200 m—23·4, 400 m—52·1, 800 m—2:01·4, 1500 m—4:26·5, mile—4:44·6, LJ—5·80/19′ 0¼″ (5·83/19′ 1½″ w).

International Championships: 1966 Commonwealth—5th 440 y (54·7). 1968 Olympics—2nd 400 m (52·1), semi-finalist 200 m (23·4), 7th 4 × 100 m (43·7). 1969 European—1st 800 m (2:01·4), 1st 4 × 400 m (3:30·8).

International Matches: (400 m) 1966—4th v France (55·9). 1967—1st (Commonwealth) v USA (52·8). 1st European Cup Semi (53·8), 1st v Hungary (54·1), 1st v Poland (54·3), 3rd (Europe) v Americas (54·6), 1st European Cup Final (53·7), 1st v West Germany (53·5). 1968—1st v Poland (53·0). 1969 2nd v USA (53·7), 1st v France (53·7). (200 m) 1968—1st v West Germany (23·5).

WAAA Titles: 1965—4 × 100 m (46·6). 1967—4 × 100 y (46·9), 4 × 220 y (1:37·6), 440 y (55·3). 1968—4 × 100 m (45·5), 4 × 200 m (1:37·7), 1st UK finisher 800 m (2:02·0).

World Records: 1968—4 × 110 y (45·0). 1969—4 × 400 m (3:37·6 and 3:30·8). 1970—4 × 800 m (8:27·0).

UK Records: 1967—4 × 200 m (1:35·9). 1968—400 m (52·1), 4 × 100 m (44·0, 43·9 and 43·7), 4 × 110 y (45·0). 1969—4 × 400 m (3:37·6, 3:36·5, 3:34·3 and 3:30·8). 1970—4 × 800 m (8:27·0).

Fastest Times: 200 m—23·4, 23·4, 23·4, 23·5, 23·5 w, 23·6, 23·6 w, 23·7, 23·8, 23·9, 23·9. 400 m—52·1, 52·5, 52·8, 52·9, 53·0, 53·5, 53·5, 53·6, 53·7, 53·7, 53·7. 800 m—2:01·4, 2:02·0, 2:04·2, 2:04·8, 2:05·1, 2:05·1, 2:05·7, 2:06·2, 2:06·8, 2:07·9, 2:07·9.

I HAVE just finished reading the biography of Lillian Board and was deeply moved by an excellently-written book. In my opinion, this book should be read, not only by sports lovers but by people who lack faith in themselves and in life.

In this age of affluence and turmoil, it is refreshing to read about a woman who dedicated her life to reach the pinnacles of her field through courage and determination and then so tragically died at such a young age. I feel that if people do read the book it will give them much inspiration and it is a great example of how someone can be so courageous in time of suffering.

Many tributes have been made to Lillian Board but one mustn't forget the wonderful inspiration of help given to her by her family, particularly her father, which is so well portrayed in the book. Without this, I am sure she wouldn't have achieved her success and have given the British public so many memorable moments. Reading the book has enlightened me on what a great person she was outside the track and how she was always cheerful to the bitter end.

I, for one, will never forget her. She set a great example to all of us. The book certainly proves this and I only hope more will be done to combat that terrible affliction known as cancer. Finally, congratulations to David Emery on his fine book.

This letter, from Mr. A. M. Gill of London, N.W.11, was published in the Evening Standard *on Wednesday, 27th October, 1971.*